Institute of Leadership
Management

su　　ies

g to
n the
e

hagement

ELSEVIER

AMSTERDAM • BOSTON • HEIDELBERG • LONDON • NEW YORK • OXFORD
PARIS • SAN DIEGO • SAN FRANCISCO • SINGAPORE • SYDNEY • TOKYO
Pergamon Flexible Learning is an imprint of Elsevier

Pergamon
Flexible
Learning

Pergamon Flexible Learning is an imprint of Elsevier
Linacre House, Jordan Hill, Oxford OX2 8DP, UK
30 Corporate Drive, Suite 400, Burlington, MA 01803, USA

First edition 1986
Second edition 1991
Third edition 1997
Fourth edition 2003
Fifth edition 2007

Editor: David Pardey

Based on material in previous editions of this work

The views expressed in this work are those of the authors and do
not necessarily reflect those of the Institute of Leadership &
Management or of the publisher

Notice
No responsibility is assumed by the publisher for any injury and/or damage to persons or
property as a matter of products liability, negligence or otherwise, or from any use or operation
of any methods, products, instructions or ideas contained in the material herein

British Library Cataloguing in Publication Data
A catalogue record for this book is available from the British Library

Library of Congress Cataloguing in Publication Data
A catalogue record for this book is available from the Library of Congress

ISBN 978-0-08-046413-8

For information on all Pergamon Flexible Learning publications
visit our website at http://books.elsevier.com

Institute of Leadership & Management
Registered Office
1 Giltspur Street
London
EC1A 9DD
Telephone: 020 7294 2470
www.i-l-m.com
ILM is part of the City & Guilds Group

Typeset by Charon Tec Ltd (A Macmillan Company), Chennai, India
www.charontec.com
Printed and bound in Great Britain

07 08 09 10 11   10 9 8 7 6 5 4 3 2 1

Contents

Contents

Reflect and review 127

Series preface

Whether you are a tutor/trainer or studying management development to further your career, Super Series provides an exciting and flexible resource to help you to achieve your goals. The fifth edition is completely new and up-to-date, and has been structured to perfectly match the Institute of Leadership & Management (ILM)'s new unit-based qualifications for first line managers. It also harmonizes with the 2004 national occupational standards in management and leadership, providing an invaluable resource for S/NVQs at Level 3 in Management.

Super Series is equally valuable for anyone tutoring or studying any management programmes at this level, whether leading to a qualification or not. Individual workbooks also support short programmes, which may be recognized by ILM as Endorsed or Development Awards, or provide the ideal way to undertake CPD activities.

For learners, coping with all the pressures of today's world, Super Series offers you the flexibility to study at your own pace to fit around your professional and other commitments. You don't need a PC or to attend classes at a specific time – choose when and where to study to suit yourself! And you will always have the complete workbook as a quick reference just when you need it.

For tutors/trainers, Super Series provides an invaluable guide to what needs to be covered, and in what depth. It also allows learners who miss occasional sessions to 'catch up' by dipping into the series.

Super Series provides unrivalled support for all those involved in first line management and supervision.

Unit specification

Title:	Motivating to perform in the workplace	Unit Ref:	M3.12
Level:	3		
Credit value:	2		

Learning outcomes *The learner will*	Assessment criteria *The learner can (in an organization with which the learner is familiar)*		
1. Understand the value of assessing performance to meet organizational and individual needs	1.1 1.2	Explain the value of formal and informal performance assessment in the workplace Identify ways that could ensure fair and objective formal assessment	
2. Know how to motivate the team to improve permormance in the workplace	2.1 2.2	Outline the factors that influence how people behave at work Explain how to apply one basic recognized theory of motivation to team members	
3. Understand the value of feedback in the workplace	3.1 3.2	Explain the importance of feedback to improve communication and performance Compare the effectiveness of different types of feedback	

Workbook introduction

1 ILM Super Series study links

This workbook addresses the issues of *Motivating to Perform in the Workplace*. Should you wish to extend your study to other Super Series workbooks covering related or different subject areas, you will find a comprehensive list at the back of this book.

2 Links to ILM qualifications

This workbook relates to the learning outcomes of Unit M3.12 Motivating to perform in the workplace from the ILM Level 3 Award, Certificate and Diploma in First Line Management.

3 Links to S/NVQs in management

This workbook relates to the following Units of the Management Standards which are used in S/NVQs in Management, as well as a range of other S/NVQs:

D6. Allocate and monitor the progress and quality of work in your area of responsibility

▪ 4 Workbook objectives

All organizations need information on how their employees are performing and developing so that the future human resource planning and budgeting needs of the organization can be met. It is also important to individuals that they are given some feedback about the work they carry out. They need to know what they do well. This motivates them and helps them to realize that their value is appreciated. They also need to know where their performance needs to be improved. If they don't know this then they cannot improve.

Appraisal systems provide the information that both organizations and individuals need to know about performance. However, the type of system and the techniques used vary considerably from one organization to the next. Indeed some organizations may have no formal performance appraisal system at all.

This workbook will also assist you to contribute effectively to the performance appraisal system used in your own organization. It will also assist you in assessing the effectiveness of your existing systems and perhaps making some recommendations for ways in which both systems and documentation could be improved.

But appraising performance is of no value if it doesn't lead to improvements in performance, and at the heart of this is the need to motivate people to perform more effectively. The workbook reviews 'classical' theory about motivation, some of it going back over 50 years. The subject is treated from several points of view: the needs of human beings (Maslow); an examination of the attitudes managers have towards employees (McGregor); motivation and 'maintenance' factors (Herzberg); the links between rewards and motivation; 'internal' motivation (Hackman and Oldham). All this theory may seem daunting, but you should not find it too difficult to follow. The intention is that by the end of the session you will have a good grasp of a number of principles that can be applied in the workplace.

Finally, we shall look at how you can use feedback to help people recognize the need to improve and also to acknowledge when performance meets or surpasses the standard expected.

4.1 Objectives

When you have worked through this workbook you will be better able to:

■ define performance appraisal, and plan and prepare for a performance appraisal interview;

■ agree performance objectives and monitor performance against objectives;

■ ask appropriate interview questions and listen to employees during interviews;

■ select appropriate methods to improve performance where necessary;

■ draw up action plans and complete appraisal documentation;

■ understand what motivates people at work;

■ apply appropriate motivational techniques for teams and individuals;

■ give and receive feedback as a means of improving performance.

5 Activity planner

The following Activities need some planning and you may want to look at them now.

Activity 17 asks you to complete a Personal Qualities Appraisal Form for one of your work team.

Activity 18 requires you to record some details about an informal or formal observation on your work team carrying out a task.

Activity 19 asks you to give some information about two occasions when you have had to examine the work of your work team.

Activity 25 questions you about any occasion when you have given a member of your work team the opportunity to assess his or her own work.

Activity 33 requires you to complete an action plan showing a development area for a member of your work team.

Activity 35 requires you to discuss with a member of your work team and agree performance ratings on the three objectives set in Activity 17.

Activity 37 suggests that you rate the telephone behaviour of a member of your work team.

Activity 38 advises you to complete a narrative appraisal report for one of your work team.

Some or all of these Activities may provide the basis of evidence for your S/NVQ portfolio. All Portfolio Activities and the Work-based assignment are signposted with this icon.

The icon states the unit to which the Portfolio Activities and Work-based assignment relate.

The Work-based assignment (on page 125) asks you to select a job you feel would benefit from job enrichment, and to develop a plan to achieve this. This can also be used for your portfolio of evidence and should be useful in helping to demonstrate your competence in ensuring that such a plan:

■ is consistent with team objectives and organizational values;

■ reflects the identified training and development needs of all personnel for whom you have responsibility;

■ is clear, relevant, realistic and takes account of team and organizational constraints;

■ is agreed with individual team members and takes account of their work activities, learning ability and personal circumstances.

In this Work-based assignment is being considered as part of the assessment for the ILM Level 3 S/NVQ in Management, this **must** be agreed in advance with your ILM Centre and external verifier. This is to ensure that the requirements of the qualification are met appropriately and that suitable assessment criteria are provided to you by your ILM Centre.

Session A
The aims and objectives of appraisal

1 Introduction

All organizations need to know how well their personnel are performing. They need a system that regularly measures achievement against set targets and identifies and remedies any shortfalls against these targets.

The number of organizations running formal appraisal systems has steadily increased over the last ten years. In fact it has been estimated that over 80 per cent of organizations have some system for formally appraising their staff. There has also been a significant increase in the number of non-managerial employees being appraised. Along with this increase in the number of people receiving appraisals there has obviously also been an increase in the number of first line managers being required to run appraisals. Never has it been more important to develop the necessary skills to ensure that appraisals are run effectively.

In this first session we will look at what is meant by appraisal, and its significance, both to the organization and to an individual. We will also look at the purpose of appraisals and examine the issues that are raised and discussed in an appraisal interview.

The personnel responsible for conducting appraisal interviews will vary from one organization to another. However, in the majority of organizations the first line manager responsible for the performance of a particular work team is the person who carries out the appraisal interview for that team. In addition to any formal system that the first line manager may be responsible for, it is also essential that informal appraisal is carried out all the time.

2 Defining performance appraisal

Performance appraisal can be defined as any procedure which helps the collecting, sharing, giving and using of information collected from, and about, people at work in order to add to their performance.

So we can say that appraisal is a tool that is used to improve an organization's performance by making better use of its people and by improving their individual performances.

Activity 1

3 mins

Jot down at least **three** ways in which you could collect, check, share, give or use information from your work team for the purpose of adding to their performance at work.

_____

_____

_____

You may have thought of many different examples, such as:

■ keeping up-to-date records;
■ monitoring progress of training programmes;
■ running briefing sessions;
■ giving instructions and making sure they are carried out;
■ giving feedback on how a particular job has been done;
■ checking time cards or overtime claims;
■ monitoring attendance.

You can see from this that appraisal is a very varied activity and is something we are involved in all the time.

In addition to the informal methods we have just described, many organizations also carry out formal performance appraisals. These often take place within the context of an annual performance appraisal interview.

3 The benefits of performance appraisal

Performance appraisal provides many benefits to both the organization and the employees concerned.

Activity 2

4 mins

List **four** benefits that you think performance appraisal could produce for a first line manager.

_____

_____

_____

_____

There are many benefits to you as a first line manager. Here are some of them.

■ It provides an opportunity for you to discuss an employee's performance at work.
■ It enables you to give positive feedback to an employee on work completed to a high standard.
■ It provides an opportunity for you to identify any training needs the employee may have.
■ It produces a record of the employee's performance at work.
■ It enables you to negotiate and agree work targets and objectives for the employee to work towards during the next period.
■ It identifies any weaknesses the employee may have and looks for ways in which performance at work can be improved.
■ It helps to clarify roles.

Many of these benefits are also benefits to the employees who are being appraised. There are, however, a few additional benefits for them to enjoy.

■ Appraisal provides employees with an opportunity to discuss their job with their manager. They are able to say how they feel about things and to talk about the future.
■ Many employees appreciate their manager showing an interest in their work and find it motivates them.
■ Receiving positive feedback on work well done helps employees to realize that the work they do is appreciated and encourages them to work even harder in the future.

4 Resistance to performance appraisal

It may appear that feedback on performance assessment is inevitably going to be critical, and that it will only be used to point out things that are not being done properly.

However, this is not true. It is usually easy to think of some way in which performance can be improved but this isn't necessarily a criticism of performance to date. The dictionary defines an appraiser as one who values, and it is important to keep that in mind.

The aim of an appraisal is not to find fault, but to weigh up and evaluate performance, and the value we put on it should be very high. The whole direction of people's future careers may be strongly influenced by their appraisal at work.

Activity 3 ·

5 mins

Jot down **three** reasons why you think people don't like having their performance appraised, and why they may resist the introduction of performance appraisal.

_____

_____

_____

_____

_____

_____

_____

_____

You have probably listed some reasons given by people in your present work-place or a previous workplace. These may include the fact that:

- they don't believe that their manager is qualified to make judgements about them;
- they fear that the information discussed will not be treated confidentially;
- they feel that their first line manager is prejudiced or biased about them;
- they think that their future within the organization may be curtailed;
- they suspect that part of the appraisal is secret;
- they consider that some aspects of performance are difficult to measure;
- they believe that the admission of any failings will have a direct bearing on salary, especially when an organization operates a system of performance-related pay (PRP).

So we have established that appraisal schemes can meet with opposition from people who don't like having performance at work assessed. The reasons we have given so far are likely to be given by the people being appraised. But what about the managers and supervisors who carry out the appraisal? Many of them may have misgivings about an appraisal system too.

Activity 4

5 mins

Now try to think of **three** reasons why managers may not like appraising their employees' performance, and may resist the introduction of performance appraisal.

_____

_____

_____

_____

_____

_____

You may have found the responses to the above activity more difficult than your responses to some of the previous activities, but here are some suggestions.

■ managers may not feel comfortable when they are put in the position of 'playing god';

■ appraisal may be time consuming and managers may believe they can make better use of their time;

■ appraisal may produce a lot of paper;

■ managers can become cynical of appraisal if there is no follow-up;

■ managers may feel that appraisal interviews can result in poorer relationships with staff afterwards;

■ managers may feel that it is very difficult to set and measure performance against objective standards;

■ trade unions may be hostile to appraisal.

In spite of the possible resistance to performance appraisal, both by first line managers carrying out appraisals and by those whose performance is appraised, many organizations do operate appraisal systems. Many employers believe that the advantages are so great that they manage to minimize the disadvantages and successfully operate a system of performance appraisal.

There are a number of things that can happen to minimize the disadvantages of performance appraisal and ensure that the system operates successfully. Some of our ideas follow.

Organizations can make sure that:

- their first line managers are well trained to run appraisals;
- there is a right of appeal against any appraisal comment or marking that the employee does not agree with;
- paperwork systems are kept to a minimum.

First line managers can make sure that they:

- ensure appraisal is an ongoing process and not something that only happens formally once a year;
- plan and prepare for interviews;
- overcome any prejudice or bias they may have;
- build up trust with the people who work for them;
- use objective standards;
- give only constructive criticism.

5 The purpose of performance appraisal

Performance appraisal has a variety of purposes which we will explore next.

Activity 5

4 mins

Write down **two** reasons why your organization might want to appraise the performance of its employees.

_____

_____

_____

_____

The table below was taken from *Performance Appraisal Revisited*, by P. Long, published by the Institute of Personnel Management. It gives the results of an investigation into the objectives that appraisers believe to be the main purposes of appraisal. The investigation involved 800 organizations.

Objective	Response (%)
To set performance objectives	81
To review past performance	98
To improve current performance	97
To assess training/development needs	97
To assess increases or new levels in salary	40
To assess future potential and promotability	71
To assist career planning decisions	75
Other	4

Overall, according to the study, the most important purposes of performance appraisal appear to be:

- to review past performance;
- to improve current performance;
- to assess training and development needs;
- to set performance objectives.

Let's look at what the person being appraised hopes to achieve from the appraisal. The goals of the individuals being appraised will, of course, vary, but possible goals are:

- to impress the manager;
- to increase the chances of a bonus payment or promotion;
- to find out what the chances of promotion are;
- to find out how their performance has been rated;
- to find out what their weaknesses are;
- to find out where they need to improve performance;
- to get help in improving performance.

Sometimes there may be a problem when the objectives of the interested parties conflict. For example, the person being appraised and the human resources department may be looking for very different outcomes. However, ideally, appraisal should be part of a continuing dialogue between all the parties concerned, not the only opportunity they have to discuss widely varying interests and objectives, and as such should not be the focus for a head-on clash. Let us suppose the worst for a moment, though, and think about the sort of conflict of interests that could be highlighted by an appraisal.

Activity 6

Write down an example of a situation where there may be a complete clash between the objectives of the person being appraised and the organization.

_____

_____

_____

_____

There are many possibilities and it's quite likely that we have thought of totally different examples, but here is one suggestion.

■ The organization may have the control of costs as one of its major objectives and will be using the appraisal system to help in this, perhaps by looking for ways of making more use of people's currently underused skills. The person being appraised may not be thinking in terms of a changed job but is hoping to secure a substantial pay rise as a result of the appraisal.

6 Aims and objectives of performance appraisal

Before starting performance appraisal it is important to be very clear about the aims of the exercise. Basically there are two areas to be appraised: the ability to perform to the requirements of the job, and behaviour in terms of attitude, attendance, timekeeping etc. We have already highlighted some of the main aims when assessing job performance. These are:

■ setting performance objectives;
■ assessing past performance and improving future performance;
■ assessing training and development needs;
■ assessing future potential;
■ determining salary;
■ developing individuals;
■ improving motivation;
■ providing job satisfaction.

We will now look at some of these in detail.

6.1 Setting performance objectives

Activity 7 · · 4 mins

Take a few minutes to consider the performance objectives that you are expected to achieve. For example, at my place of work my manager expects me to turn around all student assignments within seven days.

Write down **two** examples of performance objectives that you expect your work team to meet in its job.

_____

_____

_____

_____

_____

We are not able to give you specific feedback on your objectives as they will vary depending on your job, but here are some examples of typical performance objectives that you might expect your work team to achieve:

■ receiving a maximum of two customer complaints each year;
■ producing one new product idea every two years;
■ meeting sales targets every three calendar months.

You may have noticed that all our examples of objectives contain performance standards that tell us 'how many', or 'how often', or 'by when'. Standards are usually expressed quantitatively, and refer to such measures as attendance, production rates and manufacturing tolerances. This means that performance is easily measured and the employee who is being appraised is able to monitor his or her improvement, so increasing his or her motivation.

There are many different ways in which people can be helped to improve their work performance. You might for example be able to help them to:

EXTENSION 1
In the book *Effective Performance Appraisals* Robert Maddux discusses the topic — what is meant by goals and standards.

■ increase productivity;
■ decrease wastage;
■ improve punctuality;
■ deal more quickly with correspondence that arrives on their desk.

Activity 8

4 mins

Think about the members of your own work team and some improvements you would like to see in its performance. Make a note of at least **three** things you would need to know before you could suggest improving performance. For example, before suggesting that it increases its work output you would need to know what its present workload is.

_____

_____

_____

_____

_____

You may have suggested that you would need the following information:

- what the measure of good performance is (i.e. the performance standard);
- what existing performance is, or was in the past;
- the nature of the work team's strengths and weaknesses;
- what it can do to improve its performance;
- what help is available, for example, training.

6.2 Assessing past performance and improving future performance

One of the best ways of improving your current and future performance at work is to learn from the recent past.

In many jobs performance objectives are very clear. For example, the objective to increase retail sales by 10 per cent over the same period as last year is clear and quantifiable.

However, in other jobs it is not clear what constitutes a satisfactory or good performance. Therefore it is essential to establish what is considered satisfactory or good performance and to gather evidence about past performance. This enables you to discuss this performance with the individual and to give feedback on the tasks that are completed well. It also makes it possible for you and the employee jointly to identify areas for improvement and to plan for the future.

6.3 Assessing training and development needs

One of the main objectives of any appraisal scheme is to focus on an employee's strengths and weaknesses, so that strengths can be highlighted and weaknesses can be remedied. Appraisal should be at the centre of training and development, giving increased understanding of the appraisee's performance.

Effective appraisal should accurately diagnose the learning needs of the appraisee, so that an effective training programme can be established.

Activity 9 · 3 mins

What makes a training programme effective? Write down **two** characteristics you think it should have, in order to be effective. Here is one to get you started.

It should be related to the job needs of the employee.

_____

_____

_____

_____

_____

_____

_____

_____

Your ideas will probably to similar to these.

- It should be related to the needs of the workplace.
- It should be designed with the support of management and the employee concerned.
- It should be realistic.

We are not suggesting that it is an easy task for two people to sit down and agree learning needs. There are many obstacles in the way of reaching agreement.

Activity 10

2 mins

Write down **one** reason why it may be difficult for employees to agree what their learning needs are with their manager.

_____

_____

You might have suggested one of the following 'obstacles'.

■ They may not want to admit to weaknesses or shortcomings in their performance.
■ They may become defensive if their manager mentions any weaknesses or shortcomings.
■ They may not trust their manager's judgement.
■ They may disagree over the different priorities.

Even though these obstacles may exist, organizations can sometimes find ways around them by, for example, training appraisers and appraisees, giving ongoing guidance and counselling, and using more objective appraisal techniques.

In Session B we will look in more detail at ways in which you can highlight and meet employees' identified training and development needs.

6.4 Assessing future potential

Organizations have to find staff to fill both short-term and long-term vacancies. Filling these vacancies may involve:

■ finding staff to do a new job;
■ finding staff to do an existing job.

The staff who fill these vacancies may be:

■ promoted from within the organization;
■ obtained from outside the organization.

Vacancies occur within organizations for a number of reasons. Here are some of the main reasons for vacancies occurring:

■ staff leaving;
■ maternity leave;
■ secondments;
■ retirements;
■ internal transfers;
■ promotions;
■ re-organization;
■ expansion.

An organization spends a lot of time planning its future direction and the use of its resources, including capital and equipment. It cannot do this properly without considering, at the same time, the future use of its most valuable resource – its employees.

Once the potential of different employees in an organization is identified, the supervisors and management must help them to realize it. If they don't, staff may lose heart and lose interest in what they are doing.

Activity 11

3 mins

Think about your future plans for your own work team. Write down **two** ways in which you can help its members to realize their potential.

_____

_____

_____

_____

There are clearly many ways in which this can be achieved. Here are five of them:

■ discussion and agreement with you;
■ planned work experience or secondment;
■ attendance on training courses;
■ completion of assignments;
■ completion of projects.

One of the major benefits of performance appraisal is that employees are likely to gain motivation and job satisfaction if they feel that their capabilities, inclinations and personal needs are being satisfied at work.

6.5 Determining salary

In some organizations there is a clear link between performance and pay, and the appraisal process is used to assist in determining salary. There are arguments for and against performance-related pay (PRP). For example, many organizations claim that PRP results in better performance from managers and gains more commitment from them in achieving business objectives. Other organizations claim that it is not helpful to work team building, and that individual employees are reluctant to discuss possible weaknesses when this may have a detrimental effect on any pay increase they may receive.

Activity 12 · 4 mins

Sharing out the money in organizations by giving pay rises often leads to conflict and difficulties. Write down **two** reasons why you think this is likely to happen.

_____

_____

_____

_____

Here are some common reasons.

- Employees often question the judgement of individual supervisors and first line managers.
- Employees believe that those who make the decisions are not in the best position to judge their performances and worth.
- Some employees may consider that they work harder than others and, therefore, deserve more money.
- Employees may believe that one incident around the time of appraisal has unfairly influenced the salary increase.
- Employees tend to compare each other's pay rises.

Organizations continually seek salary review procedures which are just and fair because they are aware that employees who are dissatisfied with salary levels are less likely to perform well.

Activity 13

Write down **two** ways in which organizations can attempt to make their salary system just and fair.

_____

_____

_____

_____

There are many ways in which organizations can do this. Here are a few common methods:

■ by using an effective appraisal system;
■ by seeking staff views on the salary system;
■ by looking at salary structures and systems in other organizations, perhaps in competing companies;
■ by attempting to establish formulae and rules to determine salary increases.

Many companies use consultants to help them establish improved salary review systems. These consultants carry out job evaluations to look at the relative demands of jobs within an organization. This is to provide a base for relating differences in pay to the different requirements of the jobs.

If appraisal is to be used to make salary review decisions, first line managers require relevant and objective information to determine how well staff have performed over a period of time.

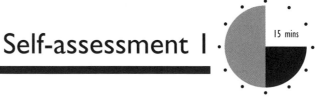

Self-assessment 1

1 Complete the following statements with a suitable word or words.

a Performance can be improved by appraisal, but that doesn't have to imply any _____ of performance to date.

b The idea of performance appraisal can meet with a lot of _____.

c Many _____ who have to appraise staff oppose appraisals.

2 List **five** main purposes or objectives of performance appraisal. (The first one has been done for you.)

    a To evaluate staff training and development needs.

    b _____

    c _____

    d _____

    e _____

    f _____

    g _____

3 Complete the following sentences with a suitable word or words.

    a We need to know certain things about the job before we can improve _____ at work.

    b Quantifying performance standards allows performance to be _____.

    c There can be problems in linking performance appraisal with _____ _____.

    d Making decisions about sharing out rewards in organizations can often lead to _____ and _____.

    e A good salary review system should attempt to be _____ and _____.

4 How can an organization ensure that it makes its system of adjusting salaries fair and just?

    _____

    _____

    _____

Answers to these questions can be found on pages 135–6.

7 Summary

- A definition of **performance appraisal** is:

  '**any procedure which helps the collecting, sharing, giving and using of information collected from and about people at work for the purposes of adding to their performance at work**'.

- The **benefits** of performance appraisal are that it gives an opportunity to:
  - discuss an individual's performance at work;
  - give positive feedback to an individual;
  - identify any training needs the individual may have;
  - produce a record of the individual's performance at work;
  - negotiate and agree work targets and objectives;
  - identify any weaknesses, and look for ways in which performance at work can be improved;
  - clarify roles;
  - discuss the job.

- **Resistance** to performance appraisal can be overcome on two fronts.

  a Organizations can make sure that:
    - their first line managers are well trained to run appraisals;
    - there is a right of appeal;
    - paperwork systems are kept to a minimum.

  b First line managers can make sure that:
    - appraisal is an ongoing process;
    - they plan and prepare for interviews;
    - they overcome any prejudice or bias they may have;
    - they build up trust with the people who work for them;
    - they use objective standards;
    - they give only constructive criticism.

- The main **aims and objectives** of appraisal are:
  - setting performance objectives;
  - assessing past and current performance;
  - improving current and future performance;
  - assessing training and development needs;
  - determining salary levels;
  - developing individuals;
  - assessing future potential;
  - improving motivation;
  - providing job satisfaction.

Session B
The appraisal process

1 Introduction

There are many kinds and varieties of performance appraisal system and yet all systems should have a number of common components if they are to be considered as quality systems.

One quality requirement is that there should be careful planning and preparation for any appraisal interview that is held. This should happen for both the first line manager and the employee. Many organizations assist employees to prepare for the interview by providing them with a pre-appraisal form to complete. This gives them time to think through the past year and to plan what they would like to discuss. It also ensures that they are not 'put on the spot' when asked searching questions by their first line manager.

Performance appraisal systems should also ensure that the appraiser collects and considers information and data that has been collected over a period of time, i.e. since the last appraisal was carried out. Although most appraisals culminate in an interview it is the information that has been gathered over time that is discussed and forms the core of the process.

It is also essential that the results of performance appraisal be recorded. A variety of systems could be used, but they should all ensure that employees have a plan for the future that they are committed to and are motivated by.

2 Planning and preparation

Before any type of interview takes place, whether the purpose be selection, appraisal or discipline, the person conducting the interview must ensure that he or she plans and prepares thoroughly.

Activity 14 · 5 mins

Imagine you are about to conduct a performance appraisal interview. What things will you need to plan and prepare for? Write your thoughts down in the space provided below.

_____

_____

_____

_____

_____

_____

The first thing you will need to be clear about is what is to be achieved in the interview. To help decide on this you may need to start by looking at what was said at the last appraisal, and perhaps complete some draft comments on an appraisal form for this year. Of course, to decide what to say on this occasion, you will need to collect evidence of present performance, and perhaps talk to other people who will have a valid view on the employee's performance. In addition to this you will need to carry out some simple tasks such as:

- agreeing a date and time for the interview with the employee;
- briefing the employee;
- booking a room for the interview;
- ensuring that there will be no interruptions.

In addition to making sure that you plan and prepare thoroughly, it is import-ant to allow time and the facilities for the employee to go through the same process. There are two main ways in which you can ensure that this happens. This is through:

■ briefing prior to the appraisal;
■ encouraging the employee to complete a pre-appraisal form (see 2.2 Pre-appraisal forms below).

2.1 Appraisal briefings

An appraisal briefing is a meeting between you and the person who is to be appraised. It should take place about one to two weeks before the actual appraisal interview. It should be an informal and fairly short meeting.

Activity 15 · 5 mins

In your opinion what should be achieved in an appraisal briefing?

_____

_____

_____

_____

_____

_____

A performance appraisal briefing should:

■ agree the date and time for the actual appraisal interview;
■ inform the employee of approximately how long the interview will last;
■ explain the purpose of the interview;
■ introduce the general topic areas that will be discussed;
■ invite the employee to add items to the agenda for discussion;
■ set his or her mind at rest;
■ allow him or her to ask any questions;
■ issue and explain the purpose of a pre-appraisal form.

2.2 Pre-appraisal forms

These forms are usually identical or very similar to the form that you will complete during the actual interview. They show the employee the questions that will be asked and the topics that will be covered.

A pre-appraisal form allows employees to plan answers to questions before the actual interview. For example, they can think about what their strengths and weaknesses are, and record examples on the form.

Allowing employees to prepare for an appraisal interview enables them to contribute well during discussions and ensures that the process is a pleasant one for them and not an ordeal.

3 Assessing performance

There are two stages to the process of assessing performance:

stage 1: gathering information about the appraisee
stage 2: the appraisal interview.

3.1 Gathering information

Before you can hold the appraisal interview, you need to find out all you can about the employee in the work context.

Activity 16

Suggest two types of information that will be useful to you when you carry out the appraisal interview.

_____

_____

_____

_____

Your suggestions might have included finding out about the employee's personal qualities and attitude to work, and his or her skill in carrying out specific tasks.

3.2 Assessing personal qualities

Early appraisal systems often concentrated totally on the attributes of the **person**. First line managers were required to comment on employees' personal characteristics. An example of such a system is shown on page 24.

More recent appraisal systems have moved away from this approach because of the difficulties associated with it, but first line managers are still frequently asked to comment on and evaluate personal characteristics.

Personal Qualities Appraisal Form						
	1	2	3	4	5	6
Performance (output and quality)						
Relations with colleagues and others						
Powers of expression						
Initiative						
Judgement						
Original thought						
Reaction to pressure						
Powers of leadership						
Ability to delegate, co-ordinate and direct						
Development of subordinates						

Overall rating [   ]   Month [   ]   Year [   ]

General comments:

Definitions:
1 Excellent
2 More than fully meets the standard for the position
3 Fully meets the standard for the position
4 Not fully up to standard required
5 Generally unsatisfactory
6 Unsatisfactory in all job aspects

Activity 17 · 15 mins

S/NVQ
D6

This Activity may provide the basis of appropriate evidence for your S/NVQ portfolio. If you are intending to take this course of action, it might be better to write your answers on separate sheets of paper.

Look at the example of the Personal Qualities Appraisal Form again and complete it for one of your work team. Having completed it, make a note of some of the difficulties you came across, or objections that you had to using this form for performance appraisal.

_____

_____

_____

_____

_____

_____

Perhaps the difficulties you thought you would have are among the following:

- It does not put any emphasis on the job itself.
- Not all the characteristics you are appraising are relevant to the job. How relevant is 'original thought' for instance, in your work team?
- It does not put any emphasis on performance.
- It is difficult to measure personal characteristics and it may be difficult to keep likes and dislikes out of your thinking.
- A personal characteristic may be considered to be a strength by one first line manager and a weakness by another.

Because this type of appraisal is based on personality traits, it is often called:

a traits-orientated approach.

Performance appraisal needs to be about performance, measured in terms of results. More recent appraisal systems have therefore tended to take:

a results-orientated approach.

3.3 Assessing job skills

Performance should be measured in terms of results.

There are a variety of techniques which can be used to assess performance but they should all compare actual performance against any performance standards or objectives set. One of your tasks as an appraiser is to ensure that evidence is gathered before the actual appraisal interview through techniques such as:

■ observing the employee;
■ examining examples of the work carried out by the employee;
■ talking to others about the employee;
■ talking directly to the employee.

This will enable you to build up an objective picture over a period of time about the work performance of the employee. You can then take this objective picture and evidence into the interview with you.

Observing the employee

As a first line manager you will be able to observe members of your work team on a regular basis. This observation can take place in passing or when you stop to check how well they are doing. You may also choose to organize some more formal performance observations. These will be planned, and your work team member will be briefed about what is to happen.

When observing employees in a more formal environment it is important that you:

■ be as unobtrusive as possible;
■ allow the employee to complete tasks in the normal work environment;
■ complete all required training before the observation takes place.

Activity 18

6 mins

S/NVQ D6

This Activity may provide the basis of appropriate evidence for your S/NVQ portfolio. If you are intending to take this course of action, it might be better to write your answers on separate sheets of paper.

Give **one** example of when you have observed, either formally or informally, one of your work team carrying out a task. Complete the form below giving details of the requested information.

Work team member:
Details of task observed:
Timing details:
Performance standards used:

Examining examples of the work carried out by the employee

For some types of work it is essential to examine a finished piece of work. Sometimes the method of achieving the work is not so important – it is the standard of the result that matters. So you do not need to spend time observing methods of work but can examine completed items only.

To ensure objective assessment you need to:

- examine a number of similar products;
- establish the start and finish time of work – this is important if the time taken to complete a task is part of the performance standard;
- compare the finished product/service against the required standards.

Activity 19

This Activity may provide the basis of appropriate evidence for your S/NVQ portfolio. If you are intending to take this course of action, it might be better to write your answers on separate sheets of paper.

Give **two** instances of work you have examined in order to form an opinion about the standards of performance of members of your work team.

Example 1	
Details of work examined:	Performance standards used:
Example 2	
Details of work examined:	Performance standards used:

4 Before the interview

Before the interview starts you must make sure that you have:

■ collected all the relevant information required during the interview;
■ set objectives for the interview and clarified these with the employee;
■ decided on the timing of the appraisal. Some organizations carry out appraisals on the anniversary of the employee's joining the company, or carry out all the staff appraisals in a relatively short space of time each year to coincide with the development of the company plan. A new employee may have more frequent appraisals, perhaps three-monthly, decreasing to yearly as performance improves;
■ allowed enough time. The appraisal interview needs adequate time to be productive and to ensure that the primary goals are achieved. There is no ideal figure for the duration of an appraisal interview but it is difficult to imagine the main objectives of an appraisal system being achieved in less than an hour.

Activity 20

Suppose you plan to carry out two appraisal interviews in a day and your diary looks like this. Where would you fit in the appraisal interviews, given that each actual interview should last about an hour?

8.00	
8.30	*Development Group meeting (about an hour)*
9.00	
9.30 9.45	*Visiting supplier (not more than 30 minutes)*
10.00	
11.00	
12.00	
12.30	*Promised to have lunch with a colleague if possible*
1.00	
1.30	*Heads of Sections meeting with manager*
2.00	
2.30	*European Market (presentation to managers, might take one and a half hours)*
3.00	
4.00	
5.00	*Staff normally finish*

You would probably have to do one in the morning, at say 10.30 a.m. when the supplier had gone, and the other in the afternoon at 4.00 p.m. You shouldn't try to squeeze two into the morning, although, at a pinch, you might have a couple of hours free.

Of course, you might have rearranged your other appointments to leave a whole day or half day as free as possible, in case the interviews take longer than anticipated. Certainly a high priority needs to be given to them. You will need to make sure that you will not be interrupted by telephone calls, visitors or other staff. You will also need to agree approximately how long you expect the interview to take.

It is important to ensure that the venue allows the appraisal interview to be carried out in a relaxed, friendly and supportive atmosphere. Even though we may not all have access to well-equipped interview rooms, there are several ways in which this kind of atmosphere can be created.

Activity 21

Write down **two** ways in which you could achieve a relaxed, friendly and supportive atmosphere.

_____

_____

_____

_____

_____

_____

Here are some suggestions.

■ Use a neutral venue – the employee is immediately at a disadvantage if the interview is on your 'territory' with you in a dominant position.

■ Use comfortable chairs – a relaxed, informal atmosphere is more easily established if you are both sitting in easy chairs rather than perched on upright ones.

■ Come out from behind your desk – if you want to talk to each other on a friendly, equal basis, you should be sitting together without any barriers between you.

■ And finally, as we have already said, make sure there are no interruptions.

5 At the start of the appraisal interview

If you are properly prepared then you can approach the actual appraisal interview feeling confident that it will be effective.

There are no hard-and-fast rules on conducting an appraisal interview, but you might find it helpful to bear the following points in mind.

5.1 Re-establish the objectives

It is important that you be clear about your objectives for the interview, and equally important that the employee should know and agree with these objectives.

If you look back to Session A you will see that there can be quite a few objectives that you may wish to achieve during the appraisal process:

■ assessing past and current performance;
■ setting performance objectives;
■ improving current and future performance;
■ assessing training and development needs;
■ determining salary levels;
■ developing individuals;
■ assessing future potential;
■ improving motivation;
■ providing job satisfaction.

It wouldn't be very helpful if your main objective were to inform employees of a salary increase, but they were expecting to discuss training and development plans for the future.

Looking back at the list of objectives for appraisal we can agree that its two main purposes are:

- to assess current performance;
- to identify ways of improving future performance.

Whatever other objectives may be discussed in any particular appraisal interview, these two key objectives must be covered.

5.2 Choose an interview style

When deciding on what interview style to use you need to consider what your normal interview style is and the type of interview you will be conducting. During an appraisal interview it is important for your style to be one that encourages the employee to talk and allows you to listen.

Activity 22

5 mins

Examine these interviewing style options.

- The **tell** option

  In this option you tell the employees what their strengths and weaknesses are and inform them of the actions that need to be taken in order to improve.

- The **tell** and **sell** option

  Here you tell the employees what their strengths and weaknesses are but also give an explanation as to why you have that opinion. When you explain what actions need to be taken in the future in order to improve you also sell the benefits to the employees.

■ The **tell** and **listen** option

In this option you again explain your own views on strengths, weaknesses and improvement action needed. However, after having explained your own point of view you allow the employees to express their own opinions too.

■ The **consultation** option

Here you first encourage the employees to explain their own views about strengths, weaknesses and improvement action needed. Having listened to what the employees have to say you decide exactly what action will take place.

■ The **joint problem-solving** option

In this option you and the employees work together to identify strengths, weakness and improvement actions required. The employees are encouraged to recommend solutions to any problems that are identified.

Which option is the one that you would choose when running an appraisal interview?

What do you consider the benefits of your chosen option to be?

_____

_____

_____

_____

_____

_____

Answers to this Activity can be found on page 140.

5.3 Keeping notes

You should explain to the employee that you are going to keep notes during the interview.

Activity 23

12 mins

What do you think is the main advantage of keeping notes during an appraisal interview?

_____

_____

_____

The advantage is that you will have a record of the main points of the interview, such as any concerns that the employee may have, new performance objectives and ideas for further training. This can then be used as a basis for discussion at the next performance review.

However, it is important to remember that the process of note-taking should not be allowed to dominate the interview.

6 During the interview

In this section we will consider a number of different skills that you will need to use during the appraisal interview. The first skill we will look at is that of encouraging the employee to talk.

6.1 Encourage the employee to talk

EXTENSION 2
The video _How Am I Doing?_ produced by Video Arts examines ways of identifying problems and opportunities during an appraisal interview. It also shows how to agree and review a plan of action.

It is important that you allow the employee to talk early on in the interview. This is so that the individual's point of view is incorporated in any conclusions drawn on his or her performance.

If the first line manager has chosen the right interview style there will be trust and openness during the interview. A warm and friendly manner will also encourage the employee to talk.

Activity 24

2 mins

Angela has worked at Myrestone for nearly twelve months and Joan Webster, her first line manager, has informed her that her first appraisal interview is due in two weeks' time. Before the interview Joan Webster had written down her views of Angela's performance over the last twelve months. Joan has always thought that Angela is one of the best employees she had ever employed.

Under the heading 'punctuality' in the appraisal report she had given a 'very poor' rating, because for the last four Mondays Angela has arrived at work up to fifteen minutes late.

Can you think of a possible reason for Angela's recent poor timekeeping?

_____

_____

_____

_____

_____

_____

_____

There may be several possible reasons, including perhaps that Angela is just becoming a poor timekeeper.

However, the real reason is that Angela's mother was an out-patient at the local hospital and was attending it for four consecutive Mondays. Angela drove her mother to the hospital and on three occasions the doctor was twenty minutes late in seeing her mother. This resulted in Angela being late for work.

Learning this at the interview, Joan Webster changed her rating to 'very good'.

The way in which you can encourage an employee to talk is by asking the right type of questions.

It is also important for you to give the employees the opportunity to comment on and assess their own work. This can be done through:

■ **Pre- or self-appraisal systems**

We covered this type of system in our section on planning and preparation and stated that it allowed employees to give some thought to their own strengths and weaknesses before the appraisal interview. This allows them to be able to answer any questions put to them by you and to state their own views and opinions clearly.

You should always ensure that the employee has had sufficient time to complete this part of the appraisal.

■ **Questions during the interview**

During the interview you should encourage employees to state their own views and opinions on the work they have carried out. You should encourage them to give specific details of work carried out and should fully explore all work issues raised.

Activity 25

S/NVQ D6

This Activity may provide the basis of appropriate evidence for your S/NVQ portfolio. If you are intending to take this course of action, it might be better to write your answers on separate sheets of paper.

Give some details below of an occasion during the performance appraisal process when you gave an individual from your work team the opportunity to assess his or her own work. (You may not be able to complete this activity if you have not yet carried out an appraisal.)

If you are compiling an S/NVQ portfolio it may be useful to ask the individual concerned to countersign your account of the occasion. This account may then form the basis of acceptable evidence.

_____

_____

_____

_____

_____

6.2 Ask questions

There are some questions where it is impossible for an employee to answer just Yes or No. These questions require them to give some information about their job or the way in which it is carried out. They require the employee to join in a discussion. These questions are called **open** questions.

Open questions usually start with the words:

- What?
- Where?
- Why?
- Who?
- When?
- How?

Activity 26

5 mins

Think of a member of your work team who will soon be interviewed by you as part of the appraisal process. Write down some open questions that you would like to ask. Try and think of at least **five** different questions.

_____

_____

_____

_____

_____

_____

_____

_____

_____

_____

It may be that an open question prompts some information from your work team member, but not in sufficient detail for appraisal purposes. It may then be necessary for you to probe a little deeper for some more information. This can be achieved by using the following methods:

- asking a follow-up question like 'Could you give me a specific example of that?';
- giving a verbal prompt using a variety of short sounds like 'Humm' or 'Ah ha' or even using silence to encourage the employee to say more;
- encouraging the employee to continue by using phrases like 'Really?' or 'Tell me more';
- repeating a key phrase from what the employee has just said, for example:

Employee:	**'That's the way it's always been.'**
First line manager:	**'Always been?'**
Employee:	**'Well certainly since last year when we ...'**

It is important for you to listen to the employees. If they feel that they have been encouraged to give their own views, and that you are listening to them with an open mind, their performance is more likely to improve.

6.3 Listen

EXTENSION 3
The Dreaded Appraisal is a Video Arts video which has key points on how to ask open questions and listen actively.

There is a well-known saying that 'The reason we have two ears and one mouth is so that we may listen more and talk less.' This saying is very relevant to an appraisal interview.

Your job in an appraisal interview is to ask sufficient questions to encourage and permit employees to talk openly and fully about their work. Having stimulated them to talk you should then **listen!**

Activity 27

4 mins

How good are you at listening? Complete the questionnaire below and rate your listening skills.

	Never	Sometimes	Always
1 I am easily distracted.			
2 I listen selectively.			
3 I get bored while others are talking.			
4 I finish other people's sentences.			
5 I interrupt other people.			
6 I maintain eye contact.			
7 I check understanding if unsure.			
8 I summarize other people's comments.			
9 I am interested in what people have to say.			
10 I am relaxed during interviews.			

Hopefully in answer to questions 1–5 you stated that you never do these things, and in answer to questions 6–10 you stated that you always do these things. If your answers differed in any way give some thought to how you can change your behaviour.

Why is it that people find listening so difficult? There are a number of reasons for this and we have included some of them below.

Managers have difficulty listening to others when:

- the views the other person holds are different from their own;
- they are being told something they do not want to hear;
- the other person speaks in long sentences;
- they start to plan what they are going to say next, even before the other person has finished talking;
- the other person has an accent or dialect;

■ the interview environment is noisy;

■ they dislike the person;

■ they are tired or under stress.

Not only is it important for you to listen effectively to what the employee is saying during the appraisal interview, it is also important to be seen to listen. The use of appropriate body language such as eye contact, smiling and nodding your head can be very useful here.

6.4 Give effective feedback

We all like to know how we are doing and how others see us. The purpose of feedback therefore is to offer information about the effect of a person's behaviour or performance. It should start a process that leads to development and change, and works best where the relationship between the giver and the receiver is already open, honest and respectful.

Feedback can be positive or negative

If given in a positive way, feedback is usually helpful in pointing out ways in which the job could have been done better, more quickly or more in line with the organization's requirements. Praise can be valuable in giving people a glow of satisfaction which makes all their hard work worthwhile. Thoughtless or harsh criticism on the other hand, can be very damaging; many people will respond by doing even less work, or taking less care.

If it is to be positive, feedback must:

■ be obviously offered for the receiver's benefit;

■ leave the receiver free to decide what to do with the information given;

■ imply an equal relationship between giver and receiver;

■ not be judgemental;

■ be expressed through 'I' statements (for example 'I thought that you found that task difficult').

We all find it easier to tell someone how wonderful they are, but what about when we need to let them know there is room for improvement? Feedback is seen as negative criticism if it:

■ demands that the other person change;

■ arises within a hierarchy (for example a senior manager has stated that he wants to see a change of behaviour);

■ is judgemental;

■ includes 'you' statements, for example 'You speak too slowly'.

Many people's experience of receiving criticism is negative or even humiliating, but it can be a good experience if done constructively.

To give constructive criticism well, it helps if you:

- plan ahead – decide exactly what you want to say, and avoid snap judgements or comments about things that cannot be changed;
- say specifically what you think is going well;
- try to give twice as much positive information as negative;
- be selective about what you say and avoid dwelling on minor details;
- be specific about what you think could be improved;
- remember to only comment on what the person does, not who the person is;
- respect the person you are talking to;
- give facts, not opinions;
- state what changes you expect and help the employees to work out how they will achieve these.

Activity 28

5 mins

Think back over last week at work. Make a list of how often you have received or given feedback or constructive criticism from and to work colleagues. Was there any time in the week when you would have found it helpful or motivating to receive more positive feedback on something you had done?

_____

_____

_____

Now think of feedback you have received, either negative or positive. What effect did it have?

_____

_____

_____

It is quite likely that you received no feedback at all. Many people go for weeks without any comment on their work so they really have no idea whether they are doing well or badly. This can only contribute to a feeling of isolation – if there is no appreciation and no attempt to acknowledge difficulties, it is almost impossible for people to improve and quite difficult to even take pride in work.

Feedback can be informal or formal

Informal feedback should be given on a regular basis as part of your everyday job as a first line manager. The more quickly you give feedback to employees about their performance, the more likely it is to influence their future performance.

Activity 29

3 mins

How regularly do you provide feedback to the members of your team about their performance? How do you think they feel about this?

_____

_____

_____

_____

If you rarely give feedback your team members are likely to feel negative and resentful about it. Conversely, if they receive frequent feedback, as long as some of it is complimentary, they will probably feel quite positive about it.

While informal feedback should be immediate, formal feedback takes longer. This is because formal feedback is often derived from such sources as:

- information gathering prior to an employee's appraisal interview;
- management reports and charts;
- production figures;
- feedback from customers.

It is important for you to pass on any formal feedback to your team because this helps to maintain morale and makes it feel an integral part of the success of the project or organization.

Activity 30

4 mins

Apart from performance appraisals, what other sources of formal feedback do you have access to that you could usefully pass on to your team?

_____

_____

_____

Whatever the formal feedback that you receive yourself, try from now on to develop a regular routine for passing on to your team any items that would be useful in their work or that would increase their motivation. There is more about using feedback to motivate people in Session F.

7 Agreeing future performance

7.1 Agreeing improvements

Before the end of the appraisal interview you must come to an agreement with the employees in three key areas:

■ areas where improved performance is required;
■ what training they might need;
■ what their future objectives are to be.

7.2 Identifying areas that need improvement

The aim of the discussions you have had during the interview is to identify areas where the employees could improve their performance. Such areas could relate to the way they do their job, their motivation or their attitude.

If both of you have been able to speak honestly and openly, the result should be a list of actions (including standards of performance) to be taken before the next appraisal. Some of these may require the acquisition of new skills or knowledge, and we will look at how this can be arranged next.

7.3 Identifying training and development needs

In Session A we agreed that effective appraisal should accurately diagnose the learning needs of employees. These needs may arise for many reasons. For example:

- changed standards or targets in an existing job;
- the introduction of new skills or tasks;
- to bring performance up to the acceptable standard.

Whatever the reason, often the appraisal process will highlight a training or development need. This means that you will need to gather information about what the employee does now and what he or she should be able to do.

In order to do this you will first need to agree performance objectives for a future period. The performance standards in these objectives may be different from those the employee has just been appraised against and you will need to discuss the reasons for this. Once the new standards have been agreed you will then need to see if the employee will require any help in order to reach the new standards. The information gathered under the section on assessing performance can be used here.

EXTENSION 4
The topic of identifying and meeting training needs through the appraisal system is covered in the book *Managing People – A Competence Approach to Supervisory Management.*

Once information has been gathered about the training need you must then give some thought to the way in which the training need is to be met.

Methods of training may include the following:

- On-the-job training

  This type of training will take place in the employee's normal working environment. It may take the form of a demonstration, coaching, counselling, mentoring, etc.

- Courses

  These courses could be organized internally or externally to the organization but will take place away from the pressures of the employee's normal working environment. Courses will usually combine different training methods: talks, discussions, videos, practical exercises, etc.

■ **Open and flexible learning**

Flexible learning could include tutor-supported open learning programmes, computer-based learning or the use of interactive videos. It might also include other types of self-developmental activities such as multimedia training or reading.

■ **Visits**

First line managers may be able to arrange visits for employees to meet and discuss issues with both customers and suppliers. It may also be possible to arrange visits to conferences and exhibitions.

■ **Projects**

Training needs can also be met by allowing employees to take on special projects. This may require them to spend time in other departments or companies, gaining additional experience and knowledge.

Activity 31

6 mins

Think of a member of your work team whose performance standards or targets you intend to change and who will need some additional training in order to meet the new standards you intend to set, and complete the form below.

Details of new objective or standard:
Training and development need(s) arising from the change:
Training method(s) to be used:

The important point is to make clear for both parties what action you agree for the future and to record it.

7.4 Agreeing an action plan

The interview should be concluded by agreeing an action plan.

Activity 32   3 mins

Make a note of **two** things that you think an action plan should contain.

_____

_____

_____

_____

An action plan should contain:

■ recommended future action;
■ the individual's training and development needs;
■ resources required;
■ the period of time concerned, e.g. six months;
■ performance targets.

The action plan on page 48 is a good example as it sets out clearly the training required and the performance objectives to be achieved. To be effective, however, it needs to be passed on to other people who can help put it into effect (the training manager, for instance), and it needs to be monitored.

Monitoring involves checking regularly to see that the training is taking place, that it is successful, and that it is as relevant and to the point as was intended.

Action Plan – John Wilson

1 Future action:

- to improve punctuality to at least 90 per cent;
- learn to log sales figures (manager to train during first week of July).

2 Development plan:

- to undertake ILM Certificate in First Line Management on afternoon release at college next September;
- to attend the next 'time management' course in the training room.

3 Resources:

- £300 to be allocated from training budget (TW to authorize).

4 Time period:

- six months.

5 Review:

- review John Wilson's performance in three calendar months.

Even if the appraisal system has a long preparation period and an effective appraisal interview, it can still fall into disrepute if the action recommended is not taken.

Activity 33

S/NVQ
D6

This Activity may provide the basis of appropriate evidence for your S/NVQ portfolio. If you are intending to take this course of action, it might be better to write your answers on separate sheets of paper.

Think of a recent action plan you may have drawn up for a member of your work team. Complete the action plan provided below. If you have not recently drawn up a suitable action plan then this Activity can be used to draw one up.

Action Plan
Future action:
Development plan:
Resources:
Time period:
Review:

The advantage in recording future action in an action plan is that at the next performance appraisal interview this action can be used as the basis for discussion and for measuring the employee's performance.

7.5 Concluding the interview

It is important at this point to check that the notes you will have taken are clear and complete. You should also summarize what has been said while the employee is still with you, and fill in anything you have missed. In many organizations you would give a copy of what has been agreed to the employee.

8 After the interview

8.1 Monitoring future performance against objectives

Once the appraisal interview is over, there is a risk that everything will settle back to how it was before, because all change requires effort. Therefore, if you fail to follow up what has been agreed during the appraisal, the employee could become demotivated and cynical about the whole appraisal process, and you could lose credibility as a manager.

So it is important for you to monitor the employee's progress towards achieving the performance objectives that have been set at the interview.

Activity 34

3 mins

What methods could you use to monitor how well the employee is progressing towards achieving the agreed objectives?

_____

_____

_____

_____

Your suggestions might have included:

■ holding regular reviews (say, every three months) during which you would discuss the employee's progress and identify any problems that may prevent achievement of the objectives;

■ encouraging the employee to give you frequent informal feedback on progress;

■ regularly observing progress by 'walking about'.

Throughout the monitoring process, you should be prepared to respond to deviations from the action plan by:

■ discussing any problems the employee is having, and identifying solutions such as providing additional resources, changing the working environment or acquiring additional information;
■ involving the employee in clarifying or amending the performance standards;
■ encouraging the employee to find his or her own solutions to the deviation;
■ arranging further training;
■ agreeing amendments to the plan if these appear necessary.

One of the most effective tools you have in helping employees to achieve their goals is to boost their confidence by providing immediate feedback and regularly praising achievement – however small this may be. There is nothing as effective in keeping people motivated as being told that they are doing a good job.

Self-assessment 2

20 mins

1 Complete the following sentences with appropriate words.

a To assess performance you need to decide _____ you are going to gather evidence.

b Many appraisal interviews take place once a _____ .

c Before an appraisal interview the appraiser should always _____ the appraisee.

d Before the interview you should gather information about the employee's _____ _____ and _____ .

2 What is pre-appraisal and what is its purpose?

_____

_____

3 What is a performance standard?

_____

_____

4   What type of information do you think an appraiser may need to collect before conducting a performance appraisal interview?

_____

_____

_____

_____

5   Complete the following statements with a suitable word or words.

a   Appraisers must ensure that they agree the _____ of an appraisal interview with the individual concerned.

b   Appraisers must ensure that they collect _____ about the employee's performance.

c   Appraisers should ensure there are no _____.

6   Complete the following statements with a suitable word or words.

a   If the appraiser is _____ _____ the appraisal interview will be more _____.

b   A first line manager carrying out an appraisal should encourage the employee to _____.

c   Both during and after the appraisal interview the employee expects _____.

d   Feedback should be _____ and _____.

7   What should be included in an action plan? In the workbook we have mentioned five things.

_____

_____

_____

_____

_____

Answers to these questions can be found on pages 136–7.

9 Summary

- When **planning and preparing** the first line manager should:

    - decide on interview aims;
    - collect evidence of present performance;
    - agree a date and time for the interview with the employee;
    - brief the employee;
    - book a room for the interview;
    - ensure that there will be no interruptions;
    - encourage the employee to complete a pre-appraisal form.

- **Before assessing performance** it will be necessary to decide upon:

    - the overall purpose of the job;
    - the key areas of the job;
    - the performance objectives.

- The two different **ways of assessing** are:

    - assessing personal qualities (traits orientated);
    - assessing job skills (results orientated).

- Different **methods of assessment** are:

    - observing the work team member;
    - examining examples of work carried out by the work team member.

- **Before the interview** it is important to:

    - collect the relevant information
    - set the interview objectives
    - decide on the timing
    - make sure there are no interruptions
    - allow enough time.

- **At the start of the interview** you should remember to:

    - re-establish the objectives;
    - choose an interviewing style;
    - prepare to make brief notes.

- **During the interview** you should:

    - encourage the individual to talk;
    - ask questions;
    - listen;
    - give effective feedback.

- **Feedback** can be formal or informal, negative or positive.

- **Agreeing future performance** includes:

    - identifying areas that need improvement;
    - identifying training and development needs;
    - agreeing an action plan.

- After an appraisal interview it is vital that you **follow up and monitor** future performance.

Session C
Assessment reports and records

1 Introduction

In Session B we looked at the following topics:

- reviewing performance against existing performance objectives;
- assessing personal qualities;
- assessing job skills;
- setting new performance objectives;
- identifying training and development needs.

We considered how important it is for you to record such information during the appraisal interview so that it can be referred to again later, perhaps at the next appraisal interview.

In this session we are going to examine the choice of formats available for recording what has happened at the interview, and who should have access to such records.

2 Recording systems

There are three basic types of recording system. They are as follows:

- comparison with objectives;
- ratings;
- narrative reports.

2.1 Comparison with objectives

If specific performance objectives have been agreed on a previous occasion it is possible for the interview to be based around these objectives. The appraisal document can record the summary of achievements against the pre-set objectives and can also allow some space for comments.

This method of recording assessments is quite objective but needs to allow space for subjective comment about such things as reasons for objectives not having been met, specific examples, and so on.

Activity 35 · 20 mins

S/NVQ D6

This Activity may provide the basis of appropriate evidence for your S/NVQ portfolio. If you are intending to take this course of action, it might be better to write your answers on separate sheets of paper.

Here is an example of a form using objective comparison.

Performance Appraisal Document

Strictly Confidential

Name _____   Appraised by _____

Job title _____   Review period _____

Appraisal date _____

Objectives set	Targets set	Performance rating*	General comments

* 1 = Exceeded objectives and targets; 2 = Met objectives and targets; 3 = small shortfall in meeting objectives and targets; 4 = Significant shortfall in meeting objectives and targets.

In the 'Objectives set' column write down three performance objectives that you have recently set for one of your team. Don't forget to include performance standards. Then discuss the achievement of each objective with the individual and agree a performance rating. Write this rating in the third column on the form, and add any comments you may wish to make.

2.2 Ratings

Rating scores permit you to rate particular aspects of an employee's performance against some form of numerical or alphabetical score. The previous example with regard to objectives is one example of a rating but two more specific examples are given here.

Behaviourally anchored rating scales (BARS)

Using this recording system you are given a series of statements or questions about performance and has to rate the appraisee on a scale (e.g. of 1–6, or A–E where 1 and A = excellent and 6 and E = unacceptable) according to each statement.

Here is an example of a BARS

ABC Company (BARS)	
Customer service	Rating
1 Answers the phone immediately	1
2 Provides helpful advice to telephone customers	3
3 Always keeps cool with angry customers	1
4 Gives priority to telephone customers over direct callers	4
5 Usually answers correspondence within two days	2

Activity 36

3 mins

Given that the rating scale on the BARS is:

1	2	3	4	5	6
excellent	very good	above average	average	poor	very poor

which customer service behaviours could be improved by the person appraised?

Clearly this person shows considerable room for improvement in providing helpful advice on the telephone (3) and giving priority to telephone customers over direct callers (4). Some improvement could be made in dealing promptly with correspondence (2), although performance in that area is already very good.

Behavioural observation scale (BOS)

This is a slightly different way of linking behaviour and ratings. As the appraiser you are given a series of statements which describe behaviour in a number of areas of a job. You are then asked to assess the employee and to indicate on a scale (e.g. of 1–6, or A–E) the extent to which the employee displays the characteristic being looked at.

The example below shows the BARS example we looked at earlier, adapted so that it is presented as a behavioural observation scale.

ABC Company (BOS)							
Customer service							
1 Answers the phone immediately							
Almost never	6	5	4	3	2	1	Almost always
2 Provides very helpful advice on the telephone							
Almost never	6	5	4	3	2	1	Almost always
3 Keeps cool with angry customers							
Almost never	6	5	4	3	2	1	Almost always
4 Gives equal consideration to both telephone callers and direct callers							
Almost never	6	5	4	3	2	1	Almost always
5 Answers correspondence within two days							
Almost never	6	5	4	3	2	1	Almost always

Activity 37

5 mins

S/NVQ
D6

This Activity may provide the basis of appropriate evidence for your S/NVQ portfolio. If you are intending to take this course of action, it might be better to write your answers on separate sheets of paper.

Probably some of the jobs of your work team include an element of telephone use (although it may not tally exactly with the areas examined in the BOS example for Customer Service). Spend a minute or two trying to rate one of your work team's telephone behaviour by circling the appropriate rating on the form.

Make a note of any difficulties you encountered when using this type of performance appraisal technique.

_____

_____

_____

_____

_____

You may have found the task quite difficult and time consuming. In this example we asked you to concentrate on only one element of a job. You would need a wide variety of forms to take everyone's job into account.

2.3 Narrative reports

This recording system allows you to express views and opinions in your own words. Usually the document gives headings to assist with subject areas. This method of recording information is usually used in conjunction with other recording methods.

Here is a typical example of the narrative section of an appraisal form.

Performance
Areas of job where performance is particularly good:
Areas of job where performance needs improving:

Activity 38

15 mins

**S/NVQ
D6**

This Activity may provide the basis of appropriate evidence for your S/NVQ portfolio. If you are intending to take this course of action, it might be better to write your answers on separate sheets of paper.

Complete the narrative report above for one of the members of your work team. In the space below record any remarks you may have about this method of recording appraisal comments.

_____

_____

_____

_____

You may have found this method of recording comments very flexible, in that it allowed you to express yourself freely. However, you may feel that this system would make comparison between staff of different sections difficult due to the subjective nature of the comments made.

We have now looked in some detail at different types of appraisal system and the different situations in which they could be used. Unfortunately a good system on its own does not guarantee that the appraisal will be effective. For a good system to work well it requires the appraiser to have the right appraisal interview skills.

3 Who should have access to appraisal records?

3.1 Access by the appraiser

EXTENSION 5
An excellent video and workbook which will prove useful to first line managers in reviewing the skills covered in this workbook is *The Empowering Appraisal* produced by BBC for Business.

If an appraisal system is open the employees being appraised see their appraisal reports and perhaps even sign the completed appraisal report. On the other hand, with a closed appraisal system, the appraisal report is secret.

There are advantages and disadvantages with a closed system. These are as follows:

■ Advantages of a closed system:

  ■ Appraisers may be more unguarded.
  ■ The organization may get a more frank assessment of its staff.
  ■ If appraisers give a poor assessment there may be less ultimate embarrassment.
  ■ There is less risk of souring the relationship between appraiser and appraisee.

■ Disadvantages of a closed system:

  ■ Employees may be suspicious.
  ■ Appraisers can make judgements without the need to justify them.
  ■ The whole atmosphere of the department or organization may be affected.
  ■ It is more difficult for employees to improve their performance if the appraisal is kept secret.

What is more, since the Data Protection Acts of 1984 and 1998 employees have a right to see the assessment if appraisal records are computerized.

The trend appears to be towards more open appraisal, as this seems to strengthen employees' commitment to appraisal as a concept.

3.2 Access by others

There may or may not be clear guidelines within your organization as to who, apart from the employees concerned, has a right to see their records. Those who have access rights might include:

- the employees' departmental head;
- the human resources department;
- members of an Employment Tribunal (in the case of a future employment dispute).

It is important to keep in mind the protection given to employees' rights under the Data Protection Acts.

Self-assessment 3

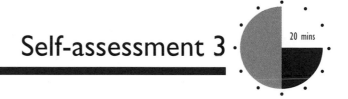

20 mins

1   In the 'comparison with objectives' recording system what two things are compared?

_____

2   What does BARS stand for?

_____

3   What does BOS stand for?

_____

4   Give three disadvantages of a closed appraisal system.

_____

_____

_____

Answers to these questions can be found on page 137.

4 Summary

- Three types of appraisal recording system are:
  - comparison with objectives;
  - ratings;
  - narrative reports.

- Appraisal systems may be open or closed.

- The Data Protection Acts give employees rights in regard to the records held about them.

Session D
What is motivation?

1 Introduction

'How many articles, books, speeches, and workshops have pleaded plaintively, "How do I get an employee to do what I want him to do?"

In lectures to industry on the problem, I have found that the audiences are anxious for quick and practical answers, so I will begin with a straightforward, practical formula for moving people. The surest and least circumlocuted way of getting someone to do something is to kick him in the pants – give him what might be called the KITA.'

Frederick Herzberg,
One More Time: How Do You Motivate Employees?

In case you are wondering whether to take these comments seriously, Frederick Herzberg went on to explain that kicking people may be one way to move them, but it is definitely **not** motivation.

Well, what is motivation? What exactly does the word mean, and why is it important to managers? How does it affect the behaviour of individuals? And to what extent is the success of organizations dependent upon the motivation of employees?

These are some of the questions we will start to look at in this session, although not all the answers will become clear until later in the workbook.

To begin with, we define the word motivation and relate it to the aims and functions of managers. Then we will look at values, attitudes and atmosphere.

This session should prepare you for the theories of motivation covered in Session E.

2 Definitions

Management tends to be all things to all people so we will start by gaining some agreement about what we **do** mean.

Activity 39 · 3 mins

How do you see your primary role as manager? Tick the one sentence below which you would say **best** describes your **main** function as a manager.

a To get a job done. ❒

b To organize and control your team so that the job which management has defined is completed satisfactorily. ❒

c To get your team to perform a task which meets the objectives of the organization. ❒

d To make it possible for the team members to get the most satisfaction from their work. ❒

e To lead your team so that defined objectives are reached and the task is carried out to the best possible ability of the team. ❒

Your response depends on how you see your role and how it has been defined for you. However, I think that:

a 'To get a job done' is too simple a definition, and suggests you do the work yourself, rather than the team doing it.

b 'To organize and control your team so that the job which management has defined is completed satisfactorily' is, on the face of things, acceptable. Organizing and controlling is frequently considered part of a manager's job. But for many teams and team leaders, 'control' is not always an appropriate word, because many teams control their own activities to a large extent. In today's working world, the manager is expected to take a less authoritarian role. As we will discuss later, this can have positive motivating effects.

In any case, this description is inadequate on the grounds that management is not usually just a question of completing a job satisfactorily. A good first line manager would have higher ambitions than that.

c 'To get your team to perform a task which meets the objectives of the organization' would certainly be close. Again though, this definition doesn't go far enough, in my opinion.

d 'To make it possible for the team members to get the most satisfaction from their work' is surely wrong – you aren't paid primarily to keep the team satisfied, though that may be a secondary objective.

e I think that 'To lead your team so that defined objectives are reached and the task is carried out to the best possible ability of the team' is the best answer. Most managers are expected to achieve the best possible results, and to get the best from the team.

This Activity leads us nearer to the subject of this workbook: getting the best from the team while achieving defined objectives.

So, when there is a job to be done, how can you, the manager, get your team to do it?

You can select people who have the necessary skills and knowledge to do the job efficiently. If the required attributes are lacking, you can train team members to acquire the skills, or you can try to design jobs so that they are compatible with the team's existing abilities. But finding ways to match people to jobs is not enough. The other factor, which will be critical in determining **how well** the job gets done, is the **motivation** of those doing the work.

There are lots of ways of getting people to carry out tasks to a desired performance level.

Activity 40

4 mins

Suppose you have a job to complete which is nearing its deadline. You need that extra effort from the team if the objective is to be reached in time. The problem is to persuade the members to concentrate that little bit harder, to make that additional endeavour.

For this situation, write down four or five different possible actions you might take. Don't worry whether you think a particular action would be successful. For instance, one action might be to beat them all with a stick until they agreed to work harder.

_____

_____

_____

_____

_____

_____

There are lots of options open to you. You could:

- use force – the KITA, perhaps;
- shout at them;
- plead with them;
- coax them by gentle persuasion;
- praise their performance so far;
- appeal to their better nature;
- stress the importance of the job;
- try to make the job more enjoyable;
- remind them of their duty;
- promise rewards – like buying them a drink;
- threaten them;
- let them know the probable results of **not** doing what you want them to, and leave them to make up their own minds.

These are only some of the possible actions you might take.

Determining which, if any, of these methods will be successful requires an understanding of human beings in general, and of those team members in particular.

2.1 Motivation

Now let's try to define the word 'motivation'. Perhaps you'd like to start by writing down your own definition.

Activity 41

3 mins

Write down, briefly, what the word 'motivation' means to you.

_____

_____

_____

_____

_____

_____

'I have a year-old Schnauzer. When it was a small puppy and I wanted it to move, I kicked it In the rear and it moved. Now that I have finished its obedience training, I hold up a dog biscuit when I want the Schnauzer to move. … I am the one who is motivated, and the dog is the one who moves. In this instance all I did was apply KITA frontally: I exerted a pull instead of a push' – Frederick Herzberg, _One More Time: How Do You Motivate Employees?_

Your answer may be included in those below. Motivation:

- means getting someone to do what you want them to do;
- is what makes us want to do something;
- is a kind of driving force which comes from within;
- is needed when we have a desire to achieve some objective;
- is an incentive to cause us to try to do something.

All these are more or less correct. Motivation has a lot to do with incentive and desire. It does **not** have much to do with threats, violence or seduction. When we say we're motivated to do something, we don't mean that we're being **made** to do it, or that we're being **enticed** to do it. We mean we **want** to do it.

To motivate somebody to do something, you have to get them to want to do it.

A definition of motivation from the _Longman Dictionary of the English Language_ is: 'A conscious or unconscious driving force that arouses and directs action towards the achievement of a desired goal.'

If we accept this definition, it gives us several things to think about:

- motivation can be conscious or unconscious, so we aren't necessarily aware of what it is that motivates us;
- motivation is a driving force, and is therefore a powerful influence – for good or ill;

■ a motivating factor will 'arouse and direct action'. This suggests that, once a person is motivated, he or she will be driven to act in a certain way. If the motivation is strong, it may not always be easy to direct and supervise these actions from outside;

■ another difficulty in a work situation may be to make the 'desired goal' coincide with the goal of the organization.

Let's look now at what does, or does not, motivate different people.

3 Values and attitudes

Rula Myers turned out for her club hockey team every week. She enjoyed playing and regarded it as a good form of exercise, but hockey wasn't really an important part of her life.

Then Rula was offered the job of Club Captain. When she accepted, she completely changed her attitude. She gave up a lot more of her spare time in order to organize matches and functions, and on the field she was like a girl inspired, becoming top goal scorer. Rula was very popular. The club had its best season ever.

Manny Tarbuck liked his job as crane operator. He enjoyed being able to manipulate and control the machinery in a very precise way. When he went home in the evening though, he forgot about work.

Then Manny was given a new job, training new people to operate the cranes. This didn't suit him at all. He got annoyed with recruits who didn't quickly get the hang of things, or who didn't work as hard as he did. And he went home at night still worrying about the job and wishing he could go back to being an operator himself.

Drew Winterton and his manager Naomi got on very well together. Drew hadn't been in the job very long and would sometimes get into difficulties. When that happened, Naomi would sit down and talk to him, asking him where he thought he had gone wrong. She wouldn't tell him what to do, but would try to get Drew to explain his own mistakes. Most of the time, he would realize how to put things right. Then Drew went back to work determined to do a better job.

When Naomi was moved to another section, a new manager took over. This man was much more direct. If Drew came to him to ask for help, he would be told: 'Look, this is how you do it – OK?' Drew would nod and walk away, feeling like an idiot. He would go back to work looking at the clock and counting the minutes to the end of the shift.

What can we learn from these examples?

In the first, Rula reacted very positively to increased responsibility: it provided her with a motivation she hadn't had before. People often surprise us with their abilities when they're given the scope to express themselves.

In the second, Manny disliked the new job given to him and would have preferred to stay where he was. Just because someone is good at a job, it doesn't mean that he or she will be good at teaching others. To get the best from people we have to develop their natural talents.

In the third situation, Drew felt he could ask Naomi for help while still retaining his pride and independence. He wanted patient guidance and help, not brusquely given instructions.

These situations highlight some of the complexity of behaviour of human beings. In the same circumstances, other people may well have reacted differently. Our values – the things we see as important and desirable – vary a great deal from person to person.

Individuals may well regard differing things as motivating and demotivating in their work situation. (Something that is 'demotivating' has the opposite effect to something that is 'motivating'.) We can say that:

people aren't all motivated – or demotivated – by the same things.

And yet, as we will see later in the workbook, it **is** possible to identify a number of 'motivators' and 'demotivators' which tend to produce similar effects in most people.

Perhaps at this point you'd like to record some of your experiences of being motivated and demotivated. Understanding what motivates and demotivates you is a good start to understanding the behaviour and reactions of others.

> '… there is no "right" theory of motivation, but only the individual and the particular circumstances.' – Charles B. Handy *Understanding Organizations.*

Activity 42

10 mins

Think about some occasion in the past which made you feel very positive about your job. What happened at work to make you feel this way?

_____

_____

_____

_____

Now try to think of some event which caused you to feel dissatisfied and rather negative about work.

_____

_____

_____

_____

Your first answer – something which made you feel positive – may have been one of the following:

- a promotion;
- a pay increase;
- a 'thank you' or pat on the back from your manager for a job well done;
- the achievement of a target by your team;
- just the satisfaction of having accomplished something you had been striving for.

These things have the same effect on most of us, although being promoted may not be seen by everyone as desirable.

It's very likely, too, that the boost to your morale in getting a pay rise didn't last very long: most people quickly seem to get used to the idea of having more money in their pockets.

What made you feel negative? Was it one of the following?

- The frustration of not achieving something?
- A loss of responsibility?
- A disagreement with your manager or with a colleague?
- Some company rule or policy that you didn't agree with?
- A threat to your job status or security?

What is certain is that the people responding to this Activity will produce a great variety of answers. Managers need to be aware that

values and attitudes to work vary a great deal.

4 The right atmosphere

One thing that does affect everyone is the ambience or atmosphere in the workplace.

Activity 43

Give your own organization and workplace marks out of ten for the following indicators of atmosphere.

In your opinion, to what extent:

Marks out of 10
(10 is perfection)

- are people generally supportive and co-operative? ☐
- is there an atmosphere of general good humour? ☐
- do people tend to communicate well at and between all levels? ☐
- is there mutual trust between most groups and most people? ☐
- do managers have an open door policy? ☐
- are people encouraged to develop their abilities? ☐
- are decisions and information shared? ☐
- is absenteeism and staff turnover low? ☐
- is the accident frequency low? ☐
- are customer complaints low? ☐

Total marks = _____ (out of 100)

Your responses will reflect the 'atmosphere' of your workplace. Rate your workplace according to the table:

0 to 30	You obviously think the atmosphere is pretty poor. If others agree with you, you have a good deal to worry about.	The lower the rating, the more there is for you and the other managers to do. Start by reading the rest of this workbook!
31 to 60	Looks like there's a lot of room for improvement.	
61 to 80	A rating at this level means that, while you feel things aren't too bad, they could be better.	
81 to 100	This is excellent. You must believe it's a good place to work.	

An open, sharing atmosphere will tend to give people the scope to develop their skills and abilities. Organizations with such an atmosphere are more likely to have employees who identify with management objectives. In fact, they're more likely to succeed.

The atmosphere in the workplace is a key factor in motivating people.

5 Clear objectives

If people work in an open, sharing atmosphere, not only will they be more likely to identify with management objectives, but they will also feel more ready to take on responsibility and make decisions. Of course, it's no good encouraging people to make their own decisions if they do not have the necessary information and skills, or do not know exactly what they should be trying to achieve. They need clear objectives, not just at the management level, but also at the individual level.

Jessica is a Section Head in the Customer Service Department of an insurance company. One day she is told that a particularly irate customer is on the phone, complaining about the treatment he has received over his attempts to claim insurance for the theft of his car. He has already made numerous phone calls over the course of several weeks, but he has still not had his claim settled and is not prepared to wait any longer. Having calmed the customer down, she looks in his folder and discovers that he has become angry for good reason. It is clear that it is two months since the car was stolen and declared to be beyond economic repair, and despite a number of phone calls by both him and Jessica's colleagues to the salvage company, the tax disk and owner's possessions have not been returned to him. Furthermore, the engineer's offer of £400 was £100 less than the going rate for a car of this make and age.

What should Jessica do? She knows that one of the objectives of her department is to settle claims within six weeks, and that one of the goals of the company is to deliver a quality service to customers. Furthermore, one of her own job objectives for this year is to reduce by 50% the number of written complaints about her department's service, and her manager has given her authority to make decisions on claims below £1000. Consequently, she tells the customer that she agrees he has been treated appallingly. She hopes he will feel happier about the situation if she increases the engineer's offer by £100 and if she immediately writes out a cheque for £250 to cover the value of the tax disk and the missing possessions. The customer accepts and Jessica is able to feel that she has achieved something.

In this example, knowing what her objectives are, and what she can make decisions about, motivates Jessica to deal efficiently with the customer complaint.

Activity 44

5 mins

Think of a recent situation in which you needed to make a decision about something.

■ What information did you need in order to make this decision?

_____

_____

_____

_____

_____

■ What management and/or personal objectives, if any, do you think you were helping to meet by making this decision?

_____

_____

_____

_____

_____

_____

The chances are that in making your decision, you did not consciously think about what objective(s) you were trying to achieve. But if you know what your objectives are, you should be able to identify a link between one of them and your decision. This of course raises the question of whether you – and the people you manage – know what your objectives are.

Self-assessment 4 · 10 mins

Fill in each blank in the following sentences with a suitable word, selected from the list below.

1 To_____ somebody to do something, you have to get them to _____ to do it.

2 Managers need to be aware that _____ and attitudes to work vary a great deal.

3 People aren't all motivated – or _____ – by the _____ things.

4 The _____ in the workplace is a _____ factor in motivating people.

ATMOSPHERE	DEMOTIVATED	KEY	MOTIVATE
SAME	VALUES	WANT	

(Questions 5 to 9). Tick those of the following statements that are **true**. Then explain briefly why they're true.

5 You can motivate people by threatening them with violence. ❑

_____

_____

6 You can motivate people by promising them rewards. ❑

_____

_____

7 Low absenteeism and high staff turnover are associated with a good atmosphere in an organization. ❑

_____

_____

8 People usually feel demotivated if they are required to make decisions. ❑

_____

_____

9 People are more likely to feel motivated if they know what their objectives are. ❑

_____

_____

Answers to these questions can be found on pages 137–8.

6 Summary

- Motivation has a lot to do with **incentive** and **desire**. It does **not** have much to do with threats, violence or seduction.

- To motivate somebody to do something, you have to get them to **want** to do it.

- A **definition of motivation** is: 'A conscious or unconscious driving force that arouses and directs action towards the achievement of a desired goal.'

- People aren't all motivated by the same things.

- The **atmosphere** in the workplace is a key factor in motivating people.

- Having **clear objectives** can help with motivation.

Session E
Understanding behaviour at work

1 Introduction

Understanding what motivates people is usually quite difficult. There is no simple formula: you can't say 'treat people like this and you'll get the best from them'.

The subject has occupied many brilliant minds over the past fifty years or so. In the next few sections we are going to look at some of the most significant theories about the behaviour of people at work.

These are:

- Abraham Maslow's theory of needs.
- Douglas McGregor's 'Theory X and Theory Y'.
- Frederick Herzberg's 'two-factor' theory.
- Expectancy theory.
- Hackman and Oldham's essential job characteristics for internal motivation.

You may feel that this is a lot to take in. However, you aren't expected to remember the names, or even which theory is which. The important thing is to understand the ideas we discuss. Then in the remainder of the workbook we can use these ideas and see how far they can be applied to your kind of workplace.

2 Maslow: needs theory

2.1 Maslow's hierarchy of needs

What are the needs of human beings? What must they have in order to be happy, successful – or even just to survive?

The American psychologist Abraham Maslow considered these questions and came to the conclusion that human needs can be thought of as being on several distinct levels:

■ **Physiological needs**. If we are starving or have other fundamental needs like air, sleep and water, we become obsessed with satisfying these needs. Anything else is irrelevant at this time.

■ **Safety needs**. Once these bodily needs are satisfied, we look for security, and stability in our environment.

■ **Love needs**. Having fed ourselves and made ourselves safe, the next level of need comes into play. The 'love' or social needs are then important to us – affection, friendship and belonging.

■ **Esteem needs**. After satisfying all these 'lower' needs, we look for esteem, self-respect and achievement.

■ **The need for self-actualization**. The final human goal is self-fulfilment – the development of our full potential in whatever field our talents lie.

We can represent Maslow's ideas in the form of a staircase diagram:

EXTENSION 6
You may like to read more about Maslow's work in Extension 6: *Effective Motivation* by John Adair, as listed on page 134.

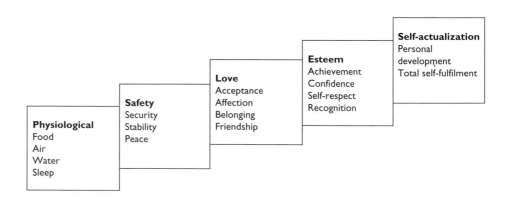

Activity 45

5 mins

State which of Maslow's 'needs categories' might be satisfied by each of the following items, by putting a tick in the appropriate column.

	Physiological	Safety	Love	Esteem	Self-actualization
A drinking fountain					
A feeling that you are attaining your career ambition.					
A comfortable working temperature.					
Meeting well the demands of your job.					
Being accepted as a valued member of a working group.					
Breathing equipment for a firefighter.					
Enjoying the respect of your manager.					

See whether you agree with my answers, which are given on page 140.

2.2 Some alternatives to Maslow's ideas

Since Maslow's work was published in the 1940s, people have looked again at the concept that human needs are arranged in a hierarchy.

In particular, Edward E. Lawler III claimed that the evidence supporting these ideas is not sufficiently convincing.

He suggested that some needs are always present, like the need for dignity and fair treatment. Other needs come and go, like hunger and the need for the company of others.

C. P. Alderfer simplified Maslow's list down to three categories:

- **existence,**
- **relating to others,** and
- **growth.**

Alderfer suggested that these three factors can operate at the same time. This rather contradicts Maslow's theory that people are aware of higher order needs only when lower order needs are satisfied.

He also put forward the idea that the less a need is fulfilled, the more important it becomes.

Answering the following questions may help you decide whether you think that Alderfer was right.

Activity 46

If someone is out of work, struggling to support a family, are they still concerned about other needs such as self-respect and love?

YES   NO

If this state of affairs gets worse, so that the person is actually starving, do other needs diminish?

YES   NO

If a person feels lacking in love and friendship, can they still want to accomplish other things?

YES   NO

My views are that:

- if you are having a hard time, you don't completely forget about the need for self-respect; also, it may be love which makes you more determined to overcome the problems and to make your family better off;
- fortunately not many of us have experienced starvation, but we can imagine that, as such basic needs get stronger, other needs would seem to be less important;
- a person lacking in love and friendship may want to satisfy that need, but may still have time and ambition to accomplish other things.

In summary, it certainly seems true that more than one level of need can exist at the same time. In addition, I would say that when a need is recognized and cannot be fulfilled, it becomes more important.

My conclusion is, therefore, that Alderfer's ideas coincide with common experience.

Of course, people look to satisfy their needs in their life as a whole, not simply at work. For instance, some people have hobbies which fulfil all their higher needs; work seems to leave them quite untouched.

Nevertheless, in this workbook we are most concerned with motivation and work, so let's examine how theories about needs relate to the workplace.

2.3 Human needs and the workplace

Because most people spend so much of their lives at work, it is important to recognize that they may regard it as more than simply a means of earning money. In fact, people in voluntary teams may not get paid at all, and yet are still motivated to perform work.

However, the usual reason why people go to work at all is to earn enough money to live – assuming they get paid for what they do. But once their income is sufficient to support them, most people look for other kinds of benefits. These aren't always tangible and may include all those things listed above.

- The need to survive is the most common reason most people go to work in the first place. Work brings the money to buy food and clothes, and to house ourselves.
- The need to interact with other human beings is often satisfied by going to work. Indeed, for some people, relationships with others is the most important thing. Being a member of a team, or working with patients, those in need, or with customers, is often a very rewarding experience. Acceptance by others is a need which is closely allied to this.
- The need to satisfy a desire to live a fuller life by helping others is clearly a motivating factor for some, and may over-ride all other considerations.
- Work often fulfils the security needs of people to some extent. Certainly the opposite seems to be true – when a person is out of paid employment, he or she may feel very insecure.
- Self-respect and a sense of achievement also seem to be very real needs. The extent to which they are fulfilled by work depends on the work being done: some work may be very unfulfilling in this respect.

■ Most of us seek recognition for our skills and abilities as well as for our accomplishments and our efforts. As we spend so much time at work, it is not surprising to find that for many people this need is satisfied only through work.

■ Many would say that the need to develop as a human being is every bit as strong as the need for, say, food and drink. Again, the amount of time we spend at work means that we look upon our work to help us satisfy this need.

3 McGregor: Theory X and Theory Y

EXTENSION 6
You can read more about McGregor's ideas in *Effective Motivation*, by John Adair, as listed on page 134.

How do managers see the behaviour of people at work?

Douglas McGregor believed that managerial decisions and actions were based on the assumptions they made about human nature and human behaviour. He wrote about his ideas in his book *The Human Side of Enterprise*.

McGregor suggested that managerial strategy was greatly influenced by a view of human nature which assumes that:

■ people inherently dislike work and will avoid it if they can;
■ because they dislike work they have to be offered rewards to work, and threatened with punishment if they don't;
■ they prefer to be controlled and directed, want to avoid responsibility, have little ambition and desire security more than anything else.

McGregor labelled this set of assumptions **Theory X.**

Activity 47

2 mins

What do you think about Theory X? Glance again at the three ideas you have just read.

a Do you think these ideas are an accurate description of people at work?

YES NO

b Do you think that managers frequently have such views of people at work?

YES NO

McGregor wrote his views in the 1950s, and they were observations of American industry. Nevertheless, you may agree with me that some managers in Britain today still seem to act as if they believed that the ideas listed in Theory X were a good description of their employees' behaviour. Fortunately, this kind of manager is less in evidence these days, as companies adopt more enlightened views. (Or perhaps you don't agree!)

I don't think that the ideas set out in Theory X are valid, in the sense of being useful and leading to high levels of motivation, and of course McGregor didn't think so either.

> 'People today are accustomed to being directed, manipulated, controlled in industrial organizations and to finding satisfaction for their social, egoistic and self-fulfilment needs away from the job. This is true of much of management as well of workers.' – McGregor, writing in 1957.

McGregor fully accepted Abraham Maslow's idea of the human needs at different levels that we discussed earlier. He went on to say that, when times were very difficult, such as in a depression, a strategy based on Theory X may be workable. When people are concerned about satisfying their needs for food and security, they are more likely to respond to the 'stick and carrot' approach suggested by Theory X.

However, according to McGregor, when we aren't living in such extreme conditions, management strategies based on these ideas lead to dissatisfaction and conflict. He thought that people needed much more from work than wages and security.

He felt that in fact, given the chance, people at work would behave quite differently from the expectations set out in Theory X. McGregor wrote down these more discerning views and labelled them **Theory Y:**

- people do not dislike work, and under the right conditions they can enjoy it;
- if they are committed to the objectives of the group, they will direct and control themselves, rather than having to be controlled from above;
- people will be committed to objectives if they are getting enough personal satisfaction from the job;
- the average human being learns to accept and to seek responsibility, if the conditions are right;
- ingenuity and creativity are widely distributed and generally under-utilized.

You probably agree that these are very different ideas to those of Theory X. McGregor saw them as being 'dynamic rather than static; they indicate the possibility of human growth, and development'.

Activity 48

You may like to give your opinions of Theory Y. Glance again at the five ideas you have just read.

Do you believe that people at work behave like this – or might behave like this if they were given the opportunity?

_____

_____

_____

_____

_____

I don't know how you may have answered this Activity. I imagine there might be a range of responses, such as:

■ 'Yes, this is exactly right. This is how people would behave if only employers would let them!'

■ 'Some people might behave like this, but I don't think all of them do. A lot of people I know behave more like Theory X.'

■ 'I accept some of the ideas of Theory Y, but not all of them.'

Even Douglas McGregor himself accepted that his ideas may in time prove to be wrong; that's why he called them theories. Theory Y does seem to have stood the test of time, nevertheless. They are seen today by many people as being perfectly valid.

Later on in the workbook we will refer back to Theory X and Theory Y when we are discussing other ideas. For the moment, I'll just remind you once more what the two theories comprise:

Theory X

● People inherently dislike work and will avoid it if they can.

● Because they dislike work they have to be offered rewards to work, and threatened with punishment if they don't.

● They prefer to be controlled and directed, want to avoid responsibility, have little ambition and desire security more than anything else.

> **Theory Y**
>
> - People do not dislike work; under the right conditions they can enjoy it.
>
> - If they are committed to the objectives of the group, they will direct and control themselves, rather than having to be controlled from above.
>
> - People will be committed to objectives if they are getting enough personal satisfaction from the job.
>
> - The average human being learns to accept and to seek responsibility, if the conditions are right.
>
> - Ingenuity and creativity are widely distributed and generally under-utilized.

4 Herzberg: the two-factor theory

Many people have found Herzberg's exploration of motivation gives them a useful insight into how people feel about their work.

Activity 49

2 mins

Without thinking about it too much, would you say that the things that motivate people are the opposite of the things that demotivate them?

| YES | NO |

You may well have said 'Yes'; many people would probably give this response. It might be argued, for example, that a wage increase would be motivating, while a decrease would be demotivating. Or if a pat on the back gives us a good feeling, a reprimand could make us feel bad.

Frederick Herzberg, another American professor of psychology, did some investigation into this subject. He asked 200 accountants and engineers to describe those times when they felt **exceptionally good** about their jobs and those times when they felt **exceptionally bad** about them.

His analysis showed that what caused the good feelings were **not** the opposite to what caused bad feelings – they were completely **different** factors.

These results were repeated in further studies involving men and women from a variety of occupations in America and Europe.

Herzberg came to the conclusion that

the factors producing job satisfaction are quite different from the factors that lead to job dissatisfaction.

Thus, there are two sets of very different factors. Herzberg called these the 'motivating' and 'maintenance' (or 'hygiene') factors. We'll look at these in turn now.

4.1 The motivating factors

Herzberg said that the five factors 'which stand out as strong determiners of job satisfaction' are

■ achievement;
■ recognition;
■ work itself;
■ responsibility;
■ advancement.

As you read my summaries of these ideas, try to decide for yourself whether you feel that what Herzberg said seems right to you.

■ **Achievement**

The personal satisfaction of completing a job, solving its problems and seeing the successful results of your own efforts.

■ **Recognition**

The acknowledgement for a job efficiently done. This may arise from within the individual or be appreciation shown by others.

■ **Work itself**

The positive effects of the job upon the person. The job may, for example, be interesting, varied, creative and challenging.

■ **Responsibility**

The degree of control a person has over the work. The amount of control that people can exercise is, in part, influenced by their authority and the responsibility that goes with it.

■ **Advancement**

The opportunity to achieve promotion within the organization. Advancement also occurs when someone is given more freedom to exercise initiative in their normal work.

Activity 50 · 2 mins

Now answer the following questions, to see how far you agree that each of these are motivating factors.

a When you have completed a difficult job to your own satisfaction, and can see the effects of what you have done, does it make you feel more positive about work?   YES   NO

b If your manager compliments you on some aspect of your work, does it usually make you feel as if you want to do even better?   YES   NO

c Do you feel more motivated when you are enjoying your work, than when you find it boring or unpleasant?   YES   NO

d If you feel that you are in control of, and responsible for, what you are doing, does this make you better motivated to do a good job?   YES   NO

e Are you motivated by the possibility of promotion, or of moving on to more interesting or more rewarding work?   YES   NO

If you answered YES, without qualification, to all these questions, then you probably agree with Herzberg's list of motivating factors.

If you didn't simply answer YES, then you disagree to some extent. There's certainly no harm in disagreeing. As you have probably realized by now, there are no hard and fast rules about this subject. In fact, it isn't a question of following a set of rules at all. How you apply motivation in your job will depend on your own understanding of the way people behave.

4.2 The maintenance factors

The factors which Herzberg found to have the effect of causing dissatisfaction, but which do not affect motivation in any positive way, are called **maintenance** factors. Another phrase that Herzberg used was 'hygiene factors'.

Maintenance factors can reduce the level of performance but not increase it. The analogy is that lack of maintenance may cause equipment to deteriorate, but regular maintenance will not improve its performance.

Activity 51

3 mins

Imagine you are happy with the job your team is doing. Working conditions are quite good. Then you learn that the building where you work has got to undergo a lot of alteration. Unfortunately, there is nowhere else for you to go and the builders have to work around your team members while they are trying to do their work. During this period tempers are frayed, absenteeism increases and output goes down. Once the building work is finished, however, things go back to normal. Output is back to its previous levels. Working conditions are better than before, although this does not have any noticeable effect on performance.

What conclusions might you draw about the effects of working conditions on performance?

_____

_____

_____

_____

_____

_____

> **The maintenance factors are:**
>
> ■ working conditions;
> ■ policy and admin;
> ■ interpersonal relationships;
> ■ salary or wages;
> ■ status;
> ■ job security.

You might reasonably conclude that working conditions don't affect the performance of the team, **provided** that they are fairly good. If the conditions become very difficult, performance **is** affected – adversely. If on the other hand working conditions become better than just **quite good**, it makes little difference to performance.

This was just the sort of result that Herzberg found. **Working conditions** is one of the maintenance factors.

I'll go through Herzberg's other maintenance factors now. This time, I'll ask you to think about each one as we come to it.

■ **Company (or organizational) policy and administration**

This means the overall operation of the organization – how it is managed and organized. If company policies conflict with the aims of groups or individuals, for example, negative consequences will result.

Activity 52   4 mins

Can you recall an occasion when a company decision or policy upset you or one of your work team? If you can, describe it very briefly.

_____

_____

_____

Do you think that lack of these kind of problems makes people better motivated?

_____

_____

_____

It is a common experience for employees to feel upset by some policy or decision made elsewhere in the company. Often, this is simply because, although the decision may be made for the good of the whole organization, some people aren't told the reason for it, even though they may be affected.

My view is that this rings true – that company policy and administration can act in a demotivating way, but that when employees don't feel affected by such things they don't think about them.

You may feel that the next of Herzberg's maintenance factors is more controversial.

■ **Supervision**

The accessibility, and social and technical competence of the manager.

Activity 53 · 3 mins

What about this one? How much are people affected by the performance of their manager – is it a maintenance factor or a motivating one? In thinking about this question, you might like to distinguish between the supervision of one person and the supervision of a team. Perhaps you could compare the relationships between you and your manager, and between your team and you.

After you've given it some thought, jot down your views in the space below.

_____

_____

_____

_____

As I said, I think that the question of whether supervision is a maintenance factor is more debatable.

Other experts have disagreed with Herzberg here. Leadership plays a very important role in motivation, especially the motivation of a team.

It may be true that you find that you – as an individual, rather than one of a team – don't spend much time thinking about your manager, until he or she is not available (or is giving you a hard time!) You may feel that you don't regard your relationship with your manager as a significant motivating factor.

Even if this is true, I wonder if the same can be said of your team's relationship with you. A work team depends on a team leader to a far greater extent, as a rule.

I don't think we can come to any firm conclusions here. Perhaps you might like to think about it some more, or discuss the question with a colleague.

The next maintenance factor, according to Herzberg, is:

■ **Interpersonal relations**

The quality of the relationships between members of the team. When they are bad, they may interfere with work; when they are good – or at least acceptable – they don't make any significant difference to behaviour.

Activity 54 ·   4 mins

To test whether you agree with this as a maintenance factor, try to recall an occasion when two team members clashed. What was the effect on their work?

_____

_____

_____

Then ask yourself whether, when people 'get along OK', they are motivated better.

_____

_____

_____

It may have not been difficult to remember an incident when conflict between people affected performance in a negative way. Perhaps we can agree that, when the quality of relationships is poor, people may become demotivated.

When it comes to good relationships, you may think that this can act in a very positive way. We've already discussed the fact that the human needs for inter-action with, and acceptance by, others are very real. To what extent good relationships are motivating is again a question for debate.

Another of Herzberg's maintenance factors is:

■ **Salary**

When you hear people say: 'So long as they keep paying me, I'm happy', then you know they aren't happy. True or false?

The income of individuals. The surprising finding of Herzberg is that wages or salary does not generally motivate people while they are doing the job, although lack of it does demotivate.

It was once thought that pay was the main motivating factor. Writing in 1911, Frederick W. Taylor said:

'… it is impossible, through any long period of time, to get workmen to work much harder than the average men around them, unless they are assured a large and permanent increase in their pay.'

Activity 55

3 mins

Say whether you agree with Taylor's statement, and briefly explain your reasoning.

_____

_____

_____

_____

_____

This is another issue which is not very straightforward. Financial reward is the main reason why most people work. But, if we are engrossed in our work and enjoy it, we may not give salary a moment's thought throughout our working day.

Pay is certainly not the only thing that motivates. However, it does become extremely important when we feel that we are underpaid – or if the company forgets to pay us! We may then feel very negative about work. If this is true, then it seems that Herzberg is right – money is a maintenance factor.

But suppose your company decides to pay your team a bonus, which is directly dependent on output or performance. Here, money is being used as a motivator.

Also, the differentials of salary may become more important than the amount of money being paid. People often seem to worry more about their earnings compared with the next person, rather than their actual salary level. Studies have shown that managers typically will believe that people above and below them are overpaid, while they themselves are underpaid. This kind of belief has a demotivating effect.

This aspect of salary brings us to the next of Herzberg's maintenance factors:

■ **Status**

This is an individual's position in relation to others. Status 'symbols', such as title, are important. A perceived reduction in status can be very demoralizing.

Activity 56

2 mins

■ Think back to the day when you were promoted to your present position. If you are honest, did you feel a little elated with your new status?   YES | NO

■ Now you are used to the idea, is the facat of your status important to your motivation to work?   YES | NO

■ If tomorrow you were demoted, so that you were no longer a manager, would this have a demotivating effect?   YES | NO

If you answered YES – NO – YES (in that order) to the questions in this Activity, then you probably agree that status is a maintenance factor, not a motivating one.

Even if you have doubts about this, perhaps you would be more ready to concede the last of the Herzberg maintenance factors:

■ **Job security**

Freedom from concern about keeping a job.

I think there is less room for argument here. I would say that most people are not normally motivated by the fact of having a job, but may become very demotivated should there be a threat of losing it.

4.3 Conclusions and criticisms

Herzberg's motivating factors:

- achievement;
- responsibility;
- the work itself;
- recognition;
- advancement;

can all be said to be one's feelings about **the job itself**. As Herzberg wrote, the motivating factors:

> 'all seem to describe man's relationship to what he does: his job content, achievement on a task, recognition for task achievement, the nature of the task, responsibility for a task and professional advancement or growth in task capability.'

Conversely, the maintenance factors:

- working conditions
- company policy and administration
- interpersonal relations
- salary
- status
- job security

> Is this all a bit too simplistic? What do you think?

can all be said to do with **the working environment**. Herzberg said of these that:

> '… the "dissatisfier" factors describe his relationship to the context or environment in which he does his job.'

Thus the first group of factors are relevant to the work a person does and the other to the environment in which it is done.

Or:

the causes of satisfaction at work lie in the content of the job; the causes of dissatisfaction lie in the working environment.

Herzberg's findings were very significant for managers. They drew attention to the fact that job content has a great influence on the behaviour of people at work, and that factors like salary and working conditions may not in themselves motivate.

However, Herzberg does have his critics.

Part of this criticism is related to Herzberg's claim that by building motivators into the job, people at work will experience job **satisfaction.**

The question is: does job satisfaction lead to high performance?

Perhaps you have your own views.

Activity 57

Do you think that a satisfied work team is a productive one?

Think about this for a few minutes and then tick the appropriate box.

YES	NO	NOT SURE

Common sense would suggest that job satisfaction and productivity go hand in hand. Yet at the same time it is difficult to argue with the following statement from *Human Resources Management* by H. T. Graham (1994), Pitman.

> 'It is possible for any degree of job satisfaction to be associated with any degree of productivity, that is, a satisfied worker may have low productivity or a dissatisfied worker may have high productivity, or vice versa.'

So it would appear that although a satisfied work team **can** be productive, it is not necessarily so.

There is no doubt that Herzberg's work has had a great deal of impact and has caused people to question traditional values. Even if you don't agree with all his findings, I hope this short synopsis has given you plenty of food for thought.

As we go through the workbook, we will refer back to Herzberg's theories.

5 Hackman and Oldham: internal motivation

J. Richard Hackman and Greg R. Oldham carried out research in the late 1970s. The work they subsequently published (in 1980) was based to some extent on the earlier theories we have discussed. However, they took a fresh approach.

Hackman and Oldham described a state of affairs in which people try to do well, because their work is rewarding and satisfying, as **internal motivation**. Their concept of the way this is achieved is shown in the following table:

The essential job characteristics:	What the worker gets from them:	The result, if all these job characteristics are present:
Feedback from job $\rightarrow$	Knowledge of the actual results of the work activities	
Autonomy $\rightarrow$	Experienced responsibility for outcomes of the work	High internal work motivation
Skill variety Task identity Task significance $\rightarrow$	Experienced meaningfulness of the work	

All the essential job characteristics must be present, Hackman and Oldham said, for there to be high internal motivation. That is, every worker needs to have:

- **feedback from the job**

People ideally need clear information about the effectiveness of their performance, directly from the job. The emphasis here is on direct feedback, as when an actor hears the audience applaud, a doctor observes a patient responding to treatment, or someone painting white lines on a football pitch sees that they're straight and visible.

Feedback may also be provided through another agent, perhaps a manager or someone else, who makes an assessment about the person's work and passes it to the worker. This indirect feedback can be valuable, too.

'Most people exhibit "motivational problems" at work when their tasks are designed so that they have little meaning, when they experience little responsibility for the work outcomes, or when they are protected from data about how well they are performing.' – J. Richard Hackman and Greg R. Oldham, 'Motivation Through the Design of Work' in Vroom and Deci, *Management and Motivation*.

Feedback provides **knowledge of the results** of the work. Workers, and teams, need to find out whether they are performing well or poorly.

■ **autonomy**

The outcome of the job should be seen by workers to be substantially dependent on their own efforts, initiatives, and decisions.

Activity 58

2 mins

Suppose you perceive that a job that you're doing depends mainly on factors you cannot control: such as the company manual, your manager, or people in another work group. Are you more, or less likely to feel responsible for the results, than if you feel that you are the one in control of the work?

More likely	Less likely

Perhaps you believe that, as your autonomy – your control over the work – increases, you will tend to accept greater **responsibility for the results**. If so, I agree with you. People generally become more willing to be accountable for the success or failure of their efforts, and for the outcome, if they have a high level of autonomy.

■ **skill variety**

This is the degree to which a job requires a variety of activities and skills. Workers who are able to perform tasks that they find challenging, and requiring more than one skill or ability, will experience meaningfulness. The more skills involved, the more meaningful the work is likely to be to them.

■ **task identity**

Task identity is the extent to which a job requires a worker to finish a complete and identifiable piece of work, i.e., a task that has a beginning and end, and a visible outcome. People care about their work more when they are doing a whole job, rather than when their work overlaps with others in an undefined way. To take a simple case, if each member of a team of cleaners is given a specified area to clean, he or she is likely to find the work more meaningful than if the entire team works together on the whole area.

■ **task significance**

This represents the amount of impact the job has on the lives of other people, whether those people are in the immediate organization or in the world at large. A nurse, who knows that the health of patients depends on his care, experiences a high degree of task significance. But if an inspector in a factory, say, is told nothing about those who subsequently sell, buy and use the product, she will experience low task significance.

These last three job characteristics – skill variety, task identity, and task significance – are essential if the worker is to **experience the work as meaningful.**

Activity 59

Test Hackman and Oldham's ideas against your own experience. Try to think of someone you know who is highly motivated; does he or she:

■ get good feedback – directly or indirectly?   YES   NO

■ have a high level of control over the work?   YES   NO

■ have the chance to apply a range of skills and abilities?   YES   NO

■ complete clearly identifiable tasks?   YES   NO

■ have a good knowledge of the significance of these tasks?   YES   NO

Now try to think of someone who does not appear to you to be well motivated, and answer the same questions about this person. Does he or she:

■ get good feedback – directly or indirectly?   YES   NO

■ have a high level of control over the work?   YES   NO

■ have the chance to apply a range of skills and abilities?   YES   NO

■ complete clearly identifiable tasks?   YES   NO

■ have a good knowledge of the significance of these tasks?   YES   NO

It seems to be a common experience that when all these job characteristics are present, motivation is high, and stays high.

Perhaps you have observed someone who seems to be well motivated, and yet you believe that some of the core characteristics of the job, listed above, are not exhibited. This most often happens when someone first takes on a job; however, almost inevitably, motivation will fall off after a while. A new recruit to a company will typically be keen to do a good job, but become disillusioned if feedback is poor, or there is little autonomy, or the job holder does not experience the work as being meaningful.

We'll take up these ideas again in Session F. Meanwhile, try the Self-assessment below.

Self-assessment 5 ·

1   Complete the diagram below by filling in with words from this list:

FOOD   STABILITY   AFFECTION
FRIENDSHIP   ACHIEVEMENT   SELF-RESPECT
PERSONAL DEVELOPMENT   ACCEPTANCE   WATER

				Self-actualization
			Esteem	————
		Love	————	Total self-fulfilment
	Safety	————	Confidence	
Physiological	Security	Belonging	————	
————	————	————	Recognition	
Air	Peace			
————				
Sleep				

2   McGregor's Theory X and Theory Y are two sets of assumptions about working people.

Which of the following statements reflect a Theory X perception of employees, and which a Theory Y? Write 'X' or 'Y' in the space provided.

Theory

a People dislike work and will avoid it whenever possible.   _____

b People, given the chance, will often exercise their
   own self-direction and self-control at work.   _____

c The average person seeks responsibility at work.   _____

d Most working people have relatively limited ambitions and prefer to be told what to do.   _____

e The best way to motivate people is to provide them with wages and job security.   _____

f The expenditure of physical and mental effort is as natural as play or rest.   _____

3 In Herzberg's two-factor theory, which of the following should be classed as motivators and which should be classed as maintenance factors? Write 'Motivator' or 'Maintenance' in the space provided:

a Acknowledgement for a job well done.   _____

b Job security.   _____

c The chance for promotion.   _____

d The opportunity to gain new knowledge.   _____

e Working conditions.   _____

f The job itself.   _____

4 In the following table, put a tick in the correct column on the right against each essential job characteristic:

The essential job characteristics:	What the worker gets from each job characteristic:		
	Knowledge of the actual results of the work activities	Experienced responsibility for outcomes of the work	Experienced meaningfulness of the work
Autonomy			
Skill variety			
Task significance			
Task identity			
Feedback from job			

Answers to these questions can be found on pages 138–9.

6 Summary

- Maslow's **hierarchy of needs** suggests that there are five sets of goals or basic needs. Only when one need is fulfilled does the next 'higher' need occupy the mind.

- McGregor's **Theory X** is the set of assumptions that people dislike work and need to be controlled and directed.

- McGregor's **Theory Y** is the idea that people will, under the right conditions, enjoy work, seek responsibility and be self-directed.

- Herzberg's **two-factor theory** indicates that the factors causing job satisfaction are not the direct opposite of those causing dissatisfaction. **Satisfaction** can be found in the **motivating factors**: achievement; recognition; work itself; responsibility; advancement. The sources of **dissatisfaction** are in the **maintenance factors**: working conditions, company policy and administration; supervision; interpersonal relations; salary; status; job security.

- Hackman and Oldham's ideas suggest that there are certain essential **job characteristics** (feedback; autonomy; skill variety; task identity; task significance) which are all necessary if a worker is to be motivated to work well.

Session F
Giving and receiving feedback

1 Introduction

The following scenario may be familiar to you.

> Kay sent out over 50 invitations for her fortieth birthday party well in advance as she wanted to know how many would be able to come in good time. On the bottom of the invitations she put RSVP (Please reply), but two weeks before the party she had still not heard from several people. Consequently, she had to spend some hours over a couple of nights ringing people up to find whether they were planning to come. How much time it would have saved – not to mention the worry of wondering if people were going to turn up – if they had bothered to reply.

All Kay needed from everyone was a few words. Without them she had no way of knowing whether her invitation had been received, what the response was going to be and whether she should continue preparing for her party. In short, what she needed was feedback.

In this session we will begin by looking at the role of feedback in establishing whether your communication has achieved its intended purpose. We will then go on to examine the role of feedback in motivating people and improving performance, focusing on how to give and receive it in regular progress and appraisal meetings.

2 The role of feedback in communication

Feedback is generally an essential part of what is called the communication process. We send a communication to someone else – the **receiver** – and in return we receive **feedback.**

2.1 The communication process

The communication process has a number of stages which involve:

- a sender;
- a communication (information or a message);
- a purpose;
- a receiver;
- an action or outcome;
- feedback.

Take a simple example.

> Ravi is the manager of a team in the company's learning centre. A manager from another department phones and asks Ellen, one of Ravi's team, if they have any learning materials on the safe use of chemicals. He has a new trainee and wants to make sure he is aware of health and safety procedures as he will be handling some quite toxic chemicals. Ellen says that they have and that she will get them ready. She suggests that the manager comes to the learning centre with the trainee and she will put together a training plan for him with the manager. The manager agrees to come up later that day. Ravi leans across to Ellen and says, 'Well done, I've been trying to get him to work with us for ages. If he comes here just once he will realize what we can do to support him.'

Activity 60 · 2 mins

Answer the following questions about this successful communication.

- Who was the sender? _____

- What was the purpose? _____

- What was the communication? _____

- Who was the receiver? _____

- What was the action or outcome? _____

- What was the feedback? _____

You should have had no difficulty in identifying those elements of the communication process. You probably also realized that communication is an out-and-back process. A sender sends a communication out to a receiver, who in turn sends one back. This return communication – feedback – tells the original sender that:

- the message has got through;
- the action, if any, has been taken;
- the purpose has been achieved.

In other words, feedback tells us whether the communication process has worked and achieved what the sender of the message set out to achieve.

The communication process therefore looks like this.

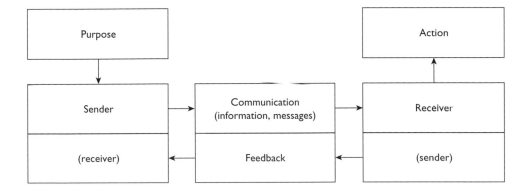

2.2 What happens without feedback?

Without feedback it's possible for all kinds of things going wrong. The simple example of Ravi and Ellen illustrates this point.

Activity 61

3 mins

In the Ravi/Ellen case study, Ravi told Ellen 'Well done' and that he had been trying for ages to get the manager to use the learning centre. If he had not done this, what might have happened?

_____

_____

Ellen had performed well, by getting the manager to use the learning centre more effectively. If Ravi had not said anything she may have wondered if that was something she was really expected to do. Next time, she might just send a learning package to the manager, as requested.

What's more, when the manager comes to the learning centre she may not realize the significance of impressing on him how much they can help him. By really making an effort, preparing well, she will do her job as well as she is able and the manager will be impressed by the service. This will encourage Ellen to perform well on future occasions. It will also support the learning centre in achieving its purpose, enabling Ravi to achieve his goals in managing it.

2.3 Feedback in meetings

Feedback can come in many different forms. For Ravi and Ellen, it was in the form of a phone conversation, but it could have been in the form of an email. In meetings – whether they are one-to-one or group meetings – it can be in the form of body language and tone of voice, as well as in the actual words that are spoken. As a manager either running or contributing to meetings, it's important that you are alert to all forms of feedback so that you can respond accordingly.

Take the following example.

Fred is the manager of the Claims Department in an insurance company. One of his staff, Marie, has been away for a couple of weeks and has not heard about the latest senior management initiative, so he arranges a meeting with her. At the agreed time she comes to his office looking a little apprehensive as she's not sure what the meeting is about. Seeing this, Fred immediately assures her that the meeting is not about anything she has, or hasn't done, but about a new customer care initiative. As he says this he notices her expression turning to one of detachment. Then, when he invites her to sit down, she immediately crosses her legs and folds her arms across her chest. Without speaking a word, the feedback she has given to Fred is that she's not very interested in the subject of customer care. If Fred doesn't find some way of engaging her interest at the outset, he will be wasting both his time and Marie's.

Activity 62

3 mins

If you were Fred, what might you do in response to the visual feedback you receive from Marie?

_____

_____

The answer depends to some extent on Fred's personality and the relationship he has with Marie. Assuming that it is normally an amicable one, he might try cracking a joke. But a safer strategy might be to ask a series of questions so that Marie has to become engaged in the meeting. He should definitely avoid just ploughing on with whatever he had planned to say. The effect would be to make a presentation to Marie rather than have a two-way discussion with her.

Now suppose Fred is invited by his manager to come to a meeting about the latest thinking on the customer care initiative.

Activity 63 · 3 mins

Fred's manager starts off the meeting by saying that the board has come up with some exciting new ideas. What body language on the part of Fred do you think would show that he is really interested in hearing about these ideas?

_____

_____

The first sign that Fred is interested might well be that he leans forward slightly. His legs might be crossed, but this won't mean he's not interested unless his arms are crossed as well. Remember – it's the combination of what people do with the different parts of their body that is important in reading body language. The same applies to facial expressions. If Fred has a frown of concentration you might take this to mean that he's not interested. You need to look at his face as a whole, and see that his expression is generally open, to get a true picture of what he's feeling.

3 Giving feedback to improve performance

Whatever the form of feedback, it can nearly always help to improve the performance of both yourself and others, and act as a significant motivator – provided, of course, that it's given properly. In fact, it's one of your responsibilities as a manager to give feedback to your staff with a view to identifying:

- ways in which their performance could be improved;
- their achievements, and how they can build on them.

You can give feedback to staff at any time, perhaps as part of your daily routine, on a completely informal basis. You can also give feedback once, or possibly twice, a year on a very formal basis, in an appraisal meeting. Between these two extremes are regular progress meetings, perhaps held on a weekly, fortnightly or monthly basis, where you sit down with staff in a one-to-one meeting to discuss how they are getting on.

We'll begin with the less formal situations and then move on to what's involved in holding an appraisal meeting.

4 Feedback in less formal situations

If you want to get a positive response to feedback, there are a number of things you should **avoid** doing, as you will see if we return to the example of Fred and Marie in the insurance company's Claims Department.

Fred regarded Marie as one of his better staff. When she spoke to customers on the phone she almost always managed to stay calm and pleasant, no matter what was being said to her.

One day Fred received a letter in which a customer complained about the way he'd been treated by Marie. Apparently, Marie had been unable to find the customer's file when he'd rung up to ask why it was taking so long for his claim to be paid. She had said she would call him back when she found the file, but she never had. Then, when the customer had called again and complained about her failure to call him, she'd been very rude to him. She had subsequently got the claim sorted out very quickly, but he felt very strongly that he should not have had to make the two phone calls.

Fred put the letter into his Complaints File and decided to speak to Marie about it later in the day. However, he was then called away to attend an urgent meeting with his manager and completely forgot about it. It was only a few days later, as he was preparing for his regular fortnightly progress meeting with Marie, that he remembered the letter of complaint and got it out ready to discuss with Marie.

The only problem was that she didn't seem to be able to remember much about this particular customer – she had dealt with so many customers since then. What's more, she obviously didn't like the way Fred started off the session by placing the customer's letter in front of her with the words: 'It seems you need to improve the way you relate to customers'. She became irritable straight away and said that the customer was probably an unpleasant piece of work who deserved everything he got.

Activity 64

3 mins

How do you think Fred should have handled this situation to get a better response from Marie to the feedback he supplied?

_____

_____

_____

Obviously it would have made a lot more sense for Fred to discuss the customer's complaint with Marie as soon as possible. Leaving it for some days meant that Marie's memory of events was blurred, thus reducing the chances of learning something from what had happened – such as how to deal in future with the type of comments the customer made.

The next mistake Fred made was to start off the meeting with a very negative comment. He would have got a more positive response if he had begun by saying something positive himself. He could, for example, have said that he was normally impressed by the way Marie dealt with difficult customers and so was wondering what had gone wrong in this particular situation. And once they had finished discussing what had gone wrong and the lessons to be learned, it would have been a good idea to remind Marie of the particular things he thought she did well.

Let's now turn to another situation in which Fred gives feedback to a member of staff.

> While Fred had been on holiday for a few days, a new member of staff, Sanjay, had joined the Claims Department. Fred hadn't had much of a chance to look at Sanjay's work, but his initial impression was that Sanjay didn't take his work seriously enough. He seemed to be forever smiling and telling jokes to his colleagues.
>
> Prior to Fred's progress meeting with Sanjay, he had a look at some of customer files that Sanjay had been working on. They nearly all seemed to be in good order, but one contained a lot of scribbled notes and was obviously incomplete.
>
> At the meeting Fred began by saying that he had a general feeling that Sanjay wasn't that interested in what he was doing. If this was indeed the case, could Sanjay tell him what it was that he didn't like? Sanjay looked

surprised at this. He thought he'd made a good start in his new job, getting on well with his colleagues and getting to grips with the paper-work. He didn't know how to answer Fred's question since he had no idea what Fred based his view of him on. There was one file that needed some sorting out, but that was all.

To Sanjay's dismay, Fred then picked up the offending file and began to talk about it as though it was typical of his work. In fact, the file was in a bit of a mess because it had been passed round between staff and temporarily mislaid: it was one of those problem cases concerning a stolen car where everything had gone wrong. The insurance company didn't even know exactly where the car was at the moment. It shouldn't have been scrapped yet, but there was a suspicion that this had in fact happened. All the scribbled notes were about conversations held that very morning with an increasingly irate customer.

Sanjay tried to start explaining all this to Fred. But Fred had decided that he needed to tell Sanjay exactly how the department operated, and that included not leaving scribbled notes in files but writing them up on the appropriate forms. It was only when he had finished that Sanjay was able to say that he had been looking forward to this meeting with Fred as he'd thought it would be an opportunity to discuss a few problems he'd been having. But perhaps that wasn't the point of progress meetings?

In fact, providing staff with the opportunity to discuss any problems they've been having is very much the point of progress meetings. Whether staff really get this opportunity will depend on the way in which you give them feedback. Instead of telling the member of staff what they should have done, or should do in a similar situation in the future, you need to ask questions and encourage a discussion of ideas and possible alternative courses of action. Fred's meeting with Sanjay would have been a lot more constructive if he had done this.

Activity 65 · 3 mins

What other mistakes do you think Fred made in giving feedback to Sanjay? Jot down two or three.

_____

_____

_____

Fred's first mistake was to jump to conclusions about Sanjay's attitude to his work, and then allow these to influence the way he talked to Sanjay in the meeting. It would have been better to have focused on what Sanjay had actually **done** rather than how he appeared. He compounded the problem by not explaining what his general impression of Sanjay was based on. Finally, by concentrating on the one file that was not as it should be, rather than pointing to all the things that were good about the other files, Fred took a very negative approach to Sanjay's work. He seemed to assume that the problems with this one file were likely to be replicated in the future, rather than trying to discover whether this was a one-off situation that was unlikely to be repeated in the future.

In short, if Fred was looking for a positive response from Sanjay, getting him to put right the things he had done wrong and feel motivated to improve his work in the future, he went entirely the wrong way about it!

4.1 Guidelines on giving feedback

The following guidelines will give you some ideas on how to provide effective feedback.

- Whenever possible, always provide feedback on a particular activity or project within a day or two of it being completed.
- Always bear in mind that negative feedback on its own generally has a bad effect. You need to balance the negative with something positive. It's usually best to start with a positive comment before saying something negative, and to end with another positive comment.
- Avoid making too many negative comments. It can end up being counter-productive, causing the other person to become defensive and bringing all useful discussion to an end. Just concentrate on a few key points.
- Ask questions with the aim of sharing ideas and exploring alternative courses of action, rather than telling the other person what you think they should do.
- Focus on what the person has **done** rather than on how they have appeared to be or what your general impression of them is.
- Focus on areas where the person is capable or improving. It will only have a demoralizing effect if you criticize them for something they can do nothing about.
- Avoid being vague. If there is a problem, make sure you are clear about what exactly the problem is.
- Don't assume that because a person has behaved in a particular way in one situation, they will always behave in this way in similar situations.

EXTENSION 7
For more detailed guidance on how to provide effective on and off-the-job feedback, take a look at *Effective Feedback Skills* by Tim Russell.

Above all, remember that the ultimate aim of feedback is to be constructive and help people to improve their performance.

Activity 66

S/NVQ D6

This Activity may provide the basis of appropriate evidence for your S/NVQ portfolio. If you are intending to take this course of action, it might be better to write your answers on separate sheets of paper.

■ How often do you give feedback to individual members of your staff, both on an entirely informal basis and during regular progress meetings? Do you intend to change this in the future, and if so, how?

_____

_____

_____

Think back to the last meeting you had with an individual member of staff in which you gave them feedback. On the basis of the guidelines listed above, in what ways do you think your feedback could have been improved?

_____

_____

_____

■ Identify a member of staff to whom you should give feedback in the near future, either as part of a regular progress meeting or at the end of a particular activity or project. How will you prepare yourself for this meeting to ensure that it is constructive? (For example: What outputs will you look at? What questions will you ask to ensure a productive discussion?)

_____

_____

_____

_____

_____

5 Receiving feedback

Asking people for feedback on your own performance – whether they are the people you manage, your colleagues, your manager, or customers – isn't difficult. Much more difficult is responding to criticism in a positive way so as not to discourage people from making any criticisms in the future.

Activity 67

- Have you ever been asked to give feedback to your own manager? If so, what critical comments, if any, did you make?

  _____

  _____

- How did your manager respond to your comments? Did the response make you feel more confident about giving further feedback in the future, or did it discourage you?

  _____

  _____

- What might your manager have done differently to encourage you to give more feedback in the future?

  _____

  _____

  There are a number of standard responses that people have to being criticized. They include:

- ignoring the criticism;
- denying the criticism has any validity;
- making excuses;
- voicing a criticism in return.

None of these responses are likely to result in a constructive dialogue on how to improve performance. Far more productive is to remain open-minded and ask the person providing the feedback to expand on what they have said. You should then be prepared to agree with the criticism if you think there is some truth to it.

Of course, there may be situations in which you think the other person's criticisms are not valid at all – or only partly valid. But even here you can avoid totally denying the criticism and lay the ground for constructive dialogue. In short, to encourage people to give you feedback you need to:

EXTENSION 8
You'll find further helpful advice on how to give and receive criticism in *Giving and Receiving Feedback: Building Constructive Communication*, by Patti Hathaway.

■ invite comments on what you do;
■ listen open-mindedly to what is said in response;
■ ask questions in a non-challenging way;
■ avoid self-justification.

Remember, you will not only get criticism when you ask for feedback. You should also get positive feedback that will highlight the things you are doing well and need to continue doing in the future. You yourself can become more motivated by feedback!

Self-assessment 6 ·

15 mins

1   Fill in the words missing from this diagram of the communication process.

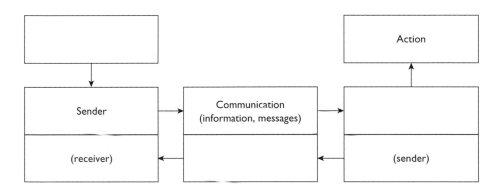

2   Why is feedback so important in the communication process?

_____

_____

For questions 3 to 6 complete the sentences about giving feedback with a suitable word from the following list. You will need to use some words more than once.

COUNTER-PRODUCTIVE   POSITIVE   DEMORALIZING
VAGUE   NEGATIVE

3   _____ feedback on its own generally has a bad effect. It's usually best to start with a _____ comment before saying something _____, and to end with another _____ comment.

4   Too many _____ comments can cause the other person to become defensive and be _____.

5   Criticizing people for something they can do nothing about will have a _____ effect.

6   Avoid being _____ about what the problems are.

7   Name at least two ways in which you can encourage people to give you feedback.

_____

_____

Answers to these questions are on pages 139–40.

6 Summary

- The communication process involves:

  - a sender;
  - a communication (information or message);
  - a purpose;
  - a receiver;
  - an action or outcome;
  - feedback.

- Feedback is important in the communication process because it tells us that the communication has worked and achieved what the sender of the message set out to achieve.

- Feedback comes in many different forms, depending on the situation. In meetings it can be in the form of body language and tone of voice, as well as in the actual words that are spoken.

- As a manager it's one of your responsibilities to give feedback to staff with a view to:

  - identifying ways in which performance could be improved;
  - recognizing their achievements, and motivating them to build on them.

- You can give feedback to staff at any time on a completely informal basis, in regular progress meetings and in six-monthly or annual appraisal meetings.

- The most important thing to remember about giving feedback is that negative criticism on its own generally has a bad effect. It's usually best to start with something positive.

- Too much negative criticism can also be counter-productive. Just concentrate on a few key points.

- In giving feedback, focus on what the person has actually done and on areas where he or she is capable of improving.

- To encourage people to give you feedback you need to:

  - invite comments on what you do;
  - listen open-mindedly to what is said in response;
  - ask questions in a non-challenging way;
  - avoid self-justification.

Performance checks

1 Quick quiz

Jot down your answers to the following questions on *Motivating to Perform in the Workplace*.

Question 1   When should first line managers assess the performance of their work teams?

_____

_____

Question 2   Why is it important for work team members to know the standard they are achieving and what is expected of them?

_____

_____

_____

Question 3   When and how often should feedback be given to a work team member about his or her work performance?

_____

_____

Question 4   Why should an effective appraisal system help an employee identify his or her training and development needs?

_____

_____

Question 5   What does the trait system of appraisal emphasize?

_____

_____

Question 6   Who else, apart from the appraisee's superior, might be interested in the out-come of appraisal?

_____

_____

Question 7   Can the appraiser be effective if he or she knows nothing about the employee's job? Give a reason for your answer.

_____

_____

Question 8   What part does preparation play in an effective appraisal interview?

_____

_____

Question 9   Suggest three methods you could use to monitor team members' performance.

_____

_____

_____

Question 10   Define the word 'motivation' in your own words.

_____

_____

Question 11   According to Maslow, there are five basic needs or goals. Esteem and self-actualization are two of them. What are the others, and in which order do they go?

_____

_____

Question 12   Theory X is a set of assumptions which McGregor thought many managers had about their employees. What approach does it suggest for getting people to do work?

_____

_____

Question 13   Theory Y is a more enlightened view than Theory X. What does it say about whether people like work or not?

_____

_____

Question 14   Looking now at Herzberg's ideas, what (briefly) is a 'maintenance factor'?

_____

_____

Question 15   According to Hackman and Oldham, which five job characteristics are essential for high internal work motivation?

_____

_____

Question 16   You can receive feedback in various forms. One form of feedback is words. Name two other forms of feedback.

_____

_____

Question 17   If you don't want to demoralize staff, there are **two** basic rules to follow in giving negative feedback. What are they?

_____

_____

Question 18   If you want to encourage people to give you feedback, you need to invite comments on what you do. Name **two** other things you should do.

_____

_____

Answers to these questions can be found on page 141.

▣ 2 Workbook assessment

Read the following case incident and then deal with the questions that follow. Write your answers on a separate sheet of paper.

Shirley is a first line manager with Holiday Premiums. Holiday Premiums is a membership organization that owns a large number of hotels, holiday homes and apartments across Europe. Members are entitled to stay at any of the properties for free, according to how many Premium Points they own. Prices for staying at each property are quoted in points, reflecting its type, category and the time that someone wants to stay. So a week in a four bedroom villa in Tuscany in August may cost 5,000 Premium Points, whereas a weekend break for two in a hotel in the Cotswolds in November may only be 100.

Shirley manages a team of eight people that organizes special events to attract members to some of the hotel properties in low season. They have quite demanding targets to achieve, and Shirley has a budget for expenditure on bought in services, such as coach trips and entry fees.

One of Shirley's team, Neil, has been doing some research into historic houses that are only open to the public on limited number of days. These houses have gained exemption from inheritance tax by opening, but do not publicize this fact. He suggest a programme of visits to 'hidden historic houses'. He says it would take some detailed planning and negotiating, but could prove to be very popular. He could go out this weekend and look at some of the places he's found that could be visited, and see if he can work out an itinerary.

Arlene, another team member groans when she hears this. 'Why can't we do something interesting?' she asks. 'Such as what?' asks Shirley. 'What about a clubbing week, or something like that, getting members VIP access to night clubs for a long weekend, or organize stag and hen parties. That would be fun!'

'Except that our members are either families with children or older people. They don't want to go clubbing and it's probably too late for them to have hen or stag parties,' Shirley replies. 'They're so boring,' says Arlene, under her breath, and turns back to her desk.

1   Using one of the theories about motivation, how would you explain both Neil and Arlene's attitude to their work?

2   What sort of feedback should Shirley use to both Neil and Arlene to motivate them? Suggest what she should say to them both.

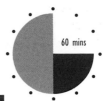

60 mins

3 Work-based assignment

S/NVQ
D6

The time guide for this assignment gives you an approximate idea of how long it is likely to take you to write up your findings. You will need to spend some additional time gathering information, perhaps talking to colleagues and thinking about the assignment.

Your written response to this assignment may form the basis of evidence for your S/NVQ portfolio.

What you have to do

1 Briefly describe the appraisal scheme which operates in your workplace. Enclose (if available) a copy of the appraisal documentation.

2 Evaluate the effectiveness of your present appraisal system in ensuring team members meet expected standards or levels of performance, and suggest ways in which it could be improved. You could use the following headings for evaluation purposes:

- Preparation and Pre-appraisal
- Appraisal of Job Skills
- Appraisal of Personal Qualities
- Assessment of Potential
- Setting of Objective Targets
- Training and Development Needs
- Action Planning
- Appraisal Documentation

3 Identify two occasions when members of your team have demonstrated both highly motivated performance and highly demotivated performance. Briefly describe each occasion, using your knowledge of motivation theory to explain why they appeared to behave as they did.

4 Describe your actions in response to their behaviour, to reinforce positive behaviour and try to counteract negative behaviour, including your use of feedback. Invite them to give their feedback on their perceptions of your performance and its effect on them.

(If your organization does not have a formal appraisal scheme describe the sort of scheme you would like to see introduced and explain why you think your choice would be appropriate.)

Reflect and review

■ 1 Reflect and review

Now that you have completed your work on *Motivating to Perform in the Workplace*, let us review our workbook objectives.

You should be better able to:

■ define performance appraisal, its aims, purposes and benefits and plan and prepare for a performance appraisal interview.

Performance appraisal can mean different things and it's important that every-one be clear about what their organization sees as being performance appraisal and that appraisal interviews are planned and prepared for. Therefore you need to consider:

■ What does your organization aim to get out of performance appraisal?

_____

_____

■ What does it see as being the benefits of performance appraisal?

_____

_____

■ What methods will you use to collect evidence on the performance of the individual?

_____

_____

- What will you include in your briefing to the individual?

  _____

  _____

- Will you use a system of pre-appraisal?

  _____

  _____

- Where will you run your appraisals and how long do you think they should last?

  _____

  _____

The second objective in the workbook was:

- to agree performance objectives and monitor performance against objectives.

  In the workbook we have tried to show you very clearly that it is essential that employees work to objective targets. This helps you review their past achievement and also helps to decide what is to be achieved in the future. Before you start setting and monitoring objectives for any of your work team you should consider the following issues.

  - How will you inform work team members of the required work standards?

    _____

    _____

  - How will you ensure that targets are jointly agreed?

    _____

    _____

  - How have team members been monitored in the past in your workplace?

    _____

    _____

  - Is there a better way of doing it which will increase the appraisees' motivation?

    _____

    _____

Another issue we looked at in this workbook was:

■ ask appropriate interview questions and listen to employees during interviews.

In order to review performance and plan for the future it is necessary to talk to the employee and gather information. This requires the first line manager to ask appropriate questions and to listen to the answers. We examined the use of open questions and how further information could be gathered through probing. As a result of this you might now like to think about the following issues.

■ How can you pre-prepare some interview questions?

_____

_____

■ At present how good are your questioning skills? How could you improve them?

_____

_____

■ How will you show the employee that you are actively listening?

_____

_____

■ How competent are you at present at listening? How could you improve these skills?

_____

_____

The next objective was:

■ to select appropriate methods to improve performance where necessary.

One of the key purposes of appraisal is to identify ways in which a team member could improve performance. With this in mind consider the following.

■ How do team members currently acquire new skills identified as a result of an appraisal?

_____

_____

■ How can you find out what other training opportunities exist to enable appraisees to acquire new skills?

_____

_____

The next objective we examined was:

■ to draw up action plans and complete appraisal documentation.

There are numerous ways in which appraisal information and findings can be recorded. We considered three main ways when we looked at comparison with objectives, ratings and narrative reporting. All the methods have advantages and disadvantages but perhaps the best system is one that combines all three and also includes an action plan. As part of your review process answer the following questions:

■ What appraisal documentation does your organization have at present?

_____

_____

■ What improvements could you make to existing documentation?

_____

_____

■ What type of action plan should you draw up at the end of your interviews?

_____

_____

■ How will you review progress?

_____

_____

The next objective we examined was:

■ to understand what motivates people at work.

Our review of motivation theory should have given you plenty to think about. Herzberg's 'two-factor theory' listed motivating factors (achievement; recognition; work itself; responsibility; advancement) and maintenance or hygiene factors (working conditions, company policy and administration; supervision; interpersonal relations; salary; status; job security). Hackman and Oldham suggested that certain core job characteristics (feedback from the job, autonomy, skill variety, task identity and task significance) are all essential for internal motivation.

Now you might like to consider how you could answer the following questions.

■ Which maintenance factors, through not being properly provided for, are tending to demotivate my team members?

_____

_____

■ Which motivation factors are missing or insufficiently provided for?

_____

_____

■ What plans am I going to make, in order to correct these deficiencies?

_____

_____

The next workbook objective was:

■ to apply appropriate motivational techniques for teams and individuals.

As we have discussed, attaining a perfect understanding of other people is next to impossible. However, the better you know the members of your team, the more you will understand their individual behaviour and what makes them work well or badly. Armed with the knowledge you have gained from this workbook, you should be better able to discover the motivation behind their behaviour.

■ What have I learned from this workbook that gives me greater insight into the behaviour of my team members? (Name at least one thing.)

_____

_____

■ What are my plans to get to know my team better?

_____

_____

The final object was that:

■ you will be better able to give and receive feedback as a means of improving performance.

■ Do you always acknowledge receiving a message or piece of information? If not, how do you decide that it's unnecessary to do so? In what sort of situations at work do you now think you should always provide feedback as part of the communication process?

_____

_____

■ Do you give enough feedback to your staff? How could you improve the way in which you give feedback so that it encourages staff to improve their performance?

_____

_____

■ What might you do to encourage your staff to give you more feedback so that you can improve your performance as a manager?

_____

_____

2 Action plan

Use the plan on page 133 to further develop for yourself a course of action you want to take. Make a note in the left-hand column of the issues or problems you want to tackle, and then decide what you intend to do, and make a note in Column 2.

The resources you need might include time, materials, information or money. You may need to negotiate for some of them, but they could be something easily acquired, like half an hour of somebody's time, or a chapter of a book. Put whatever you need in Column 3. No plan means anything without a timescale, so put a realistic target completion date in Column 4.

Finally, describe the outcome you want to achieve as a result of this plan, whether it is for your own benefit or advancement, or a more efficient way of doing things.

Desired outcomes			
1 Issues	2 Action	3 Resources	4 Target completion
Actual outcomes			

3 Extensions

Extension 1

Book	*Effective Performance Appraisals*
Author	Robert B. Maddux
Publisher	Kogan Page, 1988

Extension 2

| Video | *How Am I Doing?* |
| Publisher | Video Arts |

Extension 3

| Video | *The Dreaded Appraisal* |
| Publisher | Video Arts |

Extension 4

Book	*Managing People* (Chapter 7)
Authors	R. Cartwright, M. Collins, G. Green and A. Candy
Publisher	Blackwell, 1998

Extension 5

| Video and workbook | *The Empowering Appraisal* |
| Publisher | BBC for Business |

Extension 6

Book	*Effective Motivation*
Editor	J. Adair
Edition	1996
Publisher	Pan

John Adair has become one of the most widely respected researchers and authors about leadership, based on the relationship between the Task, the Team and the Individual. This book presents a careful evaluation of the research into motivation by people like Maslow, McGregor and Herzberg, and Adair's proposals for motivating high-performance teams.

Extension 7

Book	*Effective Feedback Skills*
Author	Tim Russell
Edition	Second edition 1998
Publisher	Kogan Page

This book provides practical guidance on the role of debriefing, on and off the job feedback, and summarizing sessions. Complete with checklists and ideas for creating a supportive training climate, the book demonstrates how to give effective feedback with tact, and shows how to deal with defensiveness.

Extension 8   Book   *Giving and Receiving Feedback: Building Constructive*
                                     Communication
                                     (A Fifty-Minute Series Book)
                     Author   Patti Hathaway
                     Edition   Revised edition 1998
                     Publisher   Crisp Publications

Few of us are good at giving or receiving criticism. This book gives advice on handling criticism and typical responses, and explains how to give meaningful criticism to others.

These Extensions can be taken up via your ILM Centre. They will either have them or will arrange that you have access to them. However, it may be more convenient to check out the materials with your personnel or training people at work – they may well give you access. There are other good reasons for approaching your own people; for example, they will become aware of your interest and you can involve them in your development.

4 Answers to self-assessment questions

Self-assessment 1 on pages 16–17

1 a Performance can be improved by appraisal, but that doesn't have to imply any **CRITICISM** of performance to date.
   b The idea of performance appraisal can meet with a lot of **OPPOSITION**.
   c Many **PEOPLE** who have to appraise staff oppose appraisals.

2 The main purposes or objectives of performance appraisal are:

   a To evaluate staff training and development needs.
   b To review past performance.
   c To improve current and future performance.
   d To assess potential.
   e To help with career planning.
   f To determine salary levels.
   g To set performance objectives.

3 a We need to know certain things about the job before we can improve **PERFORMANCE** at work.
   b Quantifying performance standards allows performance to be **MEASURED**.
   c There can be problems in linking performance appraisal with **SALARY DECISIONS**.

d Making decisions about sharing out rewards in organizations can often lead to **CONFLICT** and **DIFFICULTIES**.

e A good salary review system should attempt to be **FAIR** and **JUST**.

4 An organization can ensure that its system of adjusting salaries is fair and just by:

■ using an effective appraisal system;

■ seeking staff views on the salary system;

■ looking at salary structures and systems in other organizations;

■ attempting to establish formulae and rules to determine salary increases.

Self-assessment 2 on pages 51–2

1 a To assess performance you need to decide HOW you are going to gather evidence.

b Many appraisal interviews take place once a YEAR.

c Before an appraisal interview the appraiser should always BRIEF the appraisee.

d Before the interview you should gather information about the employee's PERSONAL QUALITIES and SKILLS.

2 Pre-appraisal is the process of briefing employees before the appraisal interview and providing them with a pre-appraisal form. The purpose is to enable them to prepare themselves for the appraisal interview.

3 A performance standard is a statement that states the standard to which a performance objective must be carried out, for example by specifying 'how many', 'how often' or 'by when'.

4 An appraiser may need to gather the following information prior to running a performance appraisal interview:

■ last year's appraisal documentation;

■ the work team member's job description;

■ a list of objectives to be achieved during the interview;

■ the views and opinions of any other interested parties;

■ information about achievement against performance objectives, e.g. sales performance against targets, etc.

5 a Appraisers must ensure that they agree the **OBJECTIVES** of an appraisal interview with the individual concerned.

b Appraisers must ensure that they collect **INFORMATION** about the appraisee's performance.

c Appraisers should ensure there are no **INTERRUPTIONS**.

6 a If the appraiser is **WELL PREPARED** the appraisal interview will be more **EFFECTIVE**.

   b A first line manager carrying out an appraisal should encourage the individual to **TALK**.

   c Both during and after the appraisal interview the individual expects **FEEDBACK**.

   d Feedback should be **QUICK** and **REGULAR**.

7 An action plan should contain:

- recommended future action;
- the individual's training and development needs;
- resources required;
- the period of time concerned, e.g. six months;
- performance targets.

Self-assessment 3 on page 63

1 The 'comparison with objectives' recording system compares current achievements with pre-set targets.

2 BARS stands for 'Behaviourally anchored rating scales'.

3 BOS stands for 'Behavioural observation scale'.

4 Employees may be suspicious, Appraisers can make judgements without having to justify them, the atmosphere of the department may be affected, it is more difficult for employees to improve their performance if the appraisal is kept secret.

Self-assessment 4 on pages 76–7

1 To MOTIVATE somebody to do something, you have to get them to WANT to do it.

2 Managers need to be aware that VALUES and attitudes to work vary a great deal.

3 People aren't all motivated – or DEMOTIVATED – by the SAME things.

4 The ATMOSPHERE in the workplace is a KEY factor in motivating people.

5 You can motivate people by threatening them with violence. This is **false**: to motivate people, you have to get them to **want** to do something, not to **have** to do something.

6 You can motivate people by promising them rewards. This is **true**, as people will want to do the job to earn the reward.

7 Low absenteeism and high staff turnover are associated with a good atmosphere in an organization. This is **false**: low absenteeism and **low** staff turnover are associated with a good atmosphere in an organization.

8   People usually feel demotivated if they are required to make decisions. This is **false**: being given the authority to make decisions in your job can be very motivating. However, this is only the case if you have adequate information and skills to make the right decisions and know what the decision is supposed to help you achieve.

9   People are more likely to feel motivated if they know what their objectives are. This is **true**: knowing what they are expected to achieve can do a great deal to motivate people.

Self-assessment 5 on pages 101–2

1   The completed diagram is:

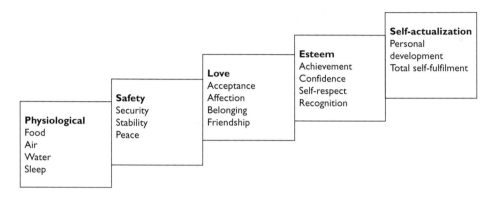

		Theory
2	a People dislike work and will avoid it whenever possible.	X
	b People, given the chance, will often exercise their own self-direction and self-control at work.	Y
	c The average person seeks responsibility at work.	Y
	d Most working people have relatively limited ambitions and prefer to be told what to do.	X
	e The best way to motivate people is to provide them with wages and job security.	X
	f The expenditure of physical and mental effort is as natural as play or rest.	Y
3	a Acknowledgement for a job well done.	MOTIVATOR
	b Job security.	MAINTENANCE
	c The chance for promotion.	MOTIVATOR
	d The opportunity to gain new knowledge.	MOTIVATOR
	e Working conditions.	MAINTENANCE
	f The job itself.	MOTIVATOR

4 The completed table is as follows:

	What the worker gets from each job characteristic:		
The essential job characteristics:	Knowledge of the actual results of the work activities	Experienced responsibility for outcomes of the work	Experienced meaningfulness of the work
Autonomy		✓	
Skill variety			✓
Task significance			✓
Task identity			✓
Feedback from job	✓		

Self-assessment 6 on pages 117–18

1 The complete diagram of the communication process is as follows.

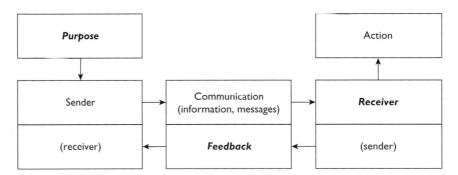

2 Feedback is important in the communication process because it tells us that the communication has worked and achieved what the sender of the message set out to achieve.

3 NEGATIVE feedback on its own generally has a bad effect. It's usually best to start with a POSITIVE comment before saying something NEGATIVE, and to end with another POSITIVE comment.

4 Too many NEGATIVE comments can cause the other person to become defensive and be DEFENSIVE.

5 Criticizing people for something they can do nothing about will have a DEMORALIZING effect.

6 Avoid being VAGUE about what the problems are.

7   Ways of encouraging people to give you feedback include:

- inviting comments on what you do;
- listening open-mindedly to what is said in response;
- asking questions in a non-challenging way;
- avoiding self-justification.

5 Answers to activities

**Activity 22
on page 33**

We hope that you selected the **joint problem-solving** option for the main style of the interview. This option has the following benefits:

- It uses the employee's own perceptions of their strengths and weaknesses and avoids any confrontation that may occur if the first line manager uses the **tell** option.
- If the employee is involved in the solution generation process they will have far more commitment to and ownership of the solutions.
- It allows the first line manager to listen to what the employee has to say before making any comments. This adds to the amount of evidence that is available to the first line manager.

**Activity 45
on page 81**

	Physiological	Safety	Love	Esteem	Self-actualization
A drinking fountain	✓				
A feeling that you are attaining your career ambition.					✓
A comfortable working temperature.	✓	✓			
Meeting well the demands of your job.				✓	
Being accepted as a valued member of a working group.			✓		
Breathing equipment for a firefighter.		✓			
Enjoying the respect of your boss.				✓	

6 Answers to the quick quiz

Answer 1   First line managers should be continuously assessing the performance of their work teams. Not just formally at the appraisal interview but all the time on a day-to-day basis.

Answer 2   It is absolutely essential for work team members to know, in quantitative terms if possible, how well they are doing with their job and the standards that their first line managers expect of them.

Answer 3   It's vital that annual appraisals provide formal feedback but feedback is also a continuous ongoing process. It's no good, for example, a first line manager waiting until a formal appraisal to tell someone that they are displeased with something that happened eleven months ago.

Answer 4   Identifying the training needs of a work team member is a very important part of an appraisal system because it helps to improve future performance.

Answer 5   This type of system concentrates on personality characteristics and traits. The idea behind this is that people need to possess certain inherent characteristics to be good at certain jobs.

Answer 6   Besides the first line manager, others who are likely to be interested in the results of an appraisal are the personnel department and senior managers.

Answer 7   No. If an appraisal system is to focus on job performance then the appraiser is likely to be much more effective if he or she knows about the job of the person being appraised.

Answer 8   Preparation plays a very important part in an appraisal interview. In order to get the best results an appraiser has to take considerable care to plan the interview properly beforehand, for example by making sure that all the necessary facts are gathered, by making sure that the interview will not be interrupted and by giving other people the chance to make a well thought out contribution.

Answer 9   Three methods you could use to monitor team members' performance are: regular reviews, encouraging them to give informal feedback on their progress, observing by 'walking about'.

Answer 10   You may have answered something like: 'Really wanting to do something', or 'Wanting to work, instead of just doing it because you have to'.

Answer 11   The Maslow list of needs, from 'lowest' to 'highest' are: physiological, safety, love, esteem and self-actualization.

Answer 12   Theory X suggests the 'stick and carrot' approach – offering money and security, and threatening people.

Answer 13 Theory Y says that people do not dislike work and under the right conditions will enjoy it.

Answer 14 A maintenance factor is something which can cause dissatisfaction when it isn't present, but will not motivate by itself.

Answer 15 They are feedback from the job, autonomy, skill variety, task identity and task significance.

Answer 16 You can receive feedback in the form of body language and tone of voice, as well as the actual words spoken.

Answer 17 If you don't want to demoralize staff, two basic rules to follow in giving negative feedback are that you balance it with something positive, and that you don't make too many negative comments.

Answer 18 Among the things you should do to encourage people to give you feedback are to:

- listen open-mindedly to what people say;
- ask questions in a non-challenging way;
- avoid self-justification.

7 Certificate

Completion of this certificate by an authorized person shows that you have worked through all the parts of this workbook and satisfactorily completed the assessments. The certificate provides a record of what you have done that may be used for exemptions or as evidence of prior learning against other nationally certificated qualifications.

superseries

Motivating to Perform in the Workplace

....

has satisfactorily completed this workbook

Name of signatory ....

Position ....

Signature ....

Date ....

Official stamp

Pergamon
Flexible
Learning

Fifth Edition

superseries

FIFTH EDITION

Workbooks in the series:

Achieving Objectives Through Time Management	978-0-08-046415-2
Building the Team	978-0-08-046412-1
Coaching and Training your Work Team	978-0-08-046418-3
Communicating One-to-One at Work	978-0-08-046438-1
Developing Yourself and Others	978-0-08-046414-5
Effective Meetings for Managers	978-0-08-046439-8
Giving Briefings and Making Presentations in the Workplace	978-0-08-046436-7
Influencing Others at Work	978-0-08-046435-0
Introduction to Leadership	978-0-08-046411-4
Managing Conflict in the Workplace	978-0-08-046416-9
Managing Creativity and Innovation in the Workplace	978-0-08-046441-1
Managing Customer Service	978-0-08-046419-0
Managing Health and Safety at Work	978-0-08-046426-8
Managing Performance	978-0-08-046429-9
Managing Projects	978-0-08-046425-1
Managing Stress in the Workplace	978-0-08-046417-6
Managing the Effective Use of Equipment	978-0-08-046432-9
Managing the Efficient Use of Materials	978-0-08-046431-2
Managing the Employment Relationship	978-0-08-046443-5
Marketing for Managers	978-0-08-046974-4
Motivating to Perform in the Workplace	978-0-08-046413-8
Obtaining Information for Effective Management	978-0-08-046434-3
Organizing and Delegating	978-0-08-046422-0
Planning Change in the Workplace	978-0-08-046444-2
Planning to Work Efficiently	978-0-08-046421-3
Providing Quality to Customers	978-0-08-046420-6
Recruiting, Selecting and Inducting New Staff in the Workplace	978-0-08-046442-8
Solving Problems and Making Decisions	978-0-08-046423-7
Understanding Change in the Workplace	978-0-08-046424-4
Understanding Culture and Ethics in Organizations	978-0-08-046428-2
Understanding Organizations in their Context	978-0-08-046427-5
Understanding the Communication Process in the Workplace	978-0-08-046433-6
Understanding Workplace Information Systems	978-0-08-046440-4
Working with Costs and Budgets	978-0-08-046430-5
Writing for Business	978-0-08-046437-4

For prices and availability please telephone our order helpline +44 (0) 1865 474010
or email   directorders@elsevier.com